THE ULTIM ATLANTIC DIET COOKBOOK

FUEL YOUR BODY, NOURISH YOUR SOUL: YOUR KEY TO LASTING WEIGHT LOSS & VIBRANT HEALTH.

EPICUREAN KITCHEN

Contents

Introduction to the Atlantic Diet

Welcome to "Healthy Atlantic Dishes," your gateway to discovering the wholesome and vibrant world of the Atlantic Diet. If you've ever dreamt of meals that not only tantalize your taste buds but also nourish your body and soul, you're in the right place. This isn't just a cookbook; it's a journey along the rugged, bountiful coasts of the Atlantic, from the sun-kissed shores of Portugal to the verdant landscapes of northern Spain, and every enchanting locale in between.

The Origins of the Atlantic Diet

The Atlantic Diet is as ancient as the ocean it's named after. Its roots delve deep into the culinary traditions of the peoples living along the Atlantic coast of Europe, especially in regions of Portugal and Galicia in Spain. This diet is a testament to the symbiotic relationship between the land, the sea, and the seasons, all of which shape the unique food culture of the Atlantic communities.

Historically, these communities were fishermen and farmers who relied on the abundance of the ocean and the fertility of their land for their daily sustenance. The Atlantic Diet evolved from this deep connection with nature, emphasizing fresh, locally sourced ingredients, simplicity in preparation, and communal eating.

Unlike other diets that have been commercialized or sensationalized, the Atlantic Diet has remained true to its roots, with recipes passed down through generations, each telling a story of the sea, the land, and the people who fish them.

Health Benefits of the Atlantic Diet

The Atlantic Diet is a celebration of all things natural and nutritious. It mirrors the Mediterranean diet in its emphasis on fresh vegetables, fruits, whole grains, legumes, and nuts, but with a stronger focus on seafood as the primary protein source. It's this rich variety of foods, brimming with life-giving nutrients, that makes the Atlantic Diet not just a way of eating, but a way of life.

Here are just a few of the myriad health benefits associated with this diet:

- **Heart Health:** The abundant use of olive oil, a staple in the Atlantic Diet, is linked to lower cholesterol levels and reduced risk of heart disease. The high intake of omega-3 fatty acids from seafood further bolsters cardiovascular health.
- **Weight Management:** Foods in the Atlantic Diet are high in fiber and nutrients but low in calories. This balance supports healthy weight management without sacrificing satisfaction or flavor.

- **Diabetes Prevention:** The diet's low glycemic index helps regulate blood sugar levels, reducing the risk of type 2 diabetes.
- **Anti-inflammatory Properties:** Omega-3 fatty acids, antioxidants, and polyphenols from the diet's cornerstone ingredients help reduce inflammation, a key factor in preventing chronic diseases.
- **Mental Health:** Emerging research suggests a diet rich in omega-3s and healthy fats can improve mental well-being and reduce the risk of depression.

How to Use This Cookbook

"Healthy Atlantic Dishes" is more than a collection of recipes; it's a guide to transforming the way you eat, cook, and think about food. Whether you're a seasoned chef or a kitchen novice, this cookbook is designed to inspire you to explore the rich flavors and simple pleasures of the Atlantic Diet.

Here's how to make the most of it:
- **Dive into the Deep End:** Don't be afraid to try new ingredients or techniques. The beauty of the Atlantic Diet lies in its diversity and adaptability. Use what's fresh, available, and appealing to you.
- **Seasonality is Key:** Pay attention to the seasons. The Atlantic Diet thrives on the principle of eating what's in season. Not only is this practice eco-friendly, but it also ensures that you're getting the most flavor and nutrition out of your ingredients.
- **Share the Love:** One of the core tenets of the Atlantic Diet is communal eating. Whenever possible, share these meals with family and friends. Food tastes better when enjoyed together, and the Atlantic Diet is all about fostering connections—both to the food and to each other.
- **Embrace Simplicity:** While some recipes might seem exotic or complex, the essence of the Atlantic Diet is simplicity. Don't get bogged down by perfection. The goal is to enjoy the process of cooking and the joy of eating wholesome, delicious food.
- **Be Mindful and Savor:** Finally, eat mindfully. The Atlantic Diet isn't just about the ingredients; it's about how you eat. Take the time to savor each bite, appreciate the flavors, and listen to your body. Eating slowly and with gratitude enhances digestion and satisfaction.

As you turn these pages, you'll find recipes that spark joy, nourish your body, and invite you to explore the rich tapestry of Atlantic culture. From the freshest seafood dishes to vibrant vegetable medleys and heartwarming whole grains, each recipe is a stepping stone on a path to wellness and a testament to the enduring appeal of the Atlantic Diet.

Welcome aboard this culinary voyage. May it bring you health, happiness, and endless delicious moments.

Part 1: The Basics of the Atlantic Kitchen

Welcome to the heart of your culinary adventure, where the robust flavors of the Atlantic meet the warmth of your kitchen. Embarking on this journey requires not just passion but also a sprinkle of knowledge and a dash of preparation. Here, we'll delve into the essentials that form the backbone of the Atlantic Diet, guiding you through the ingredients and tools you'll need, alongside pearls of wisdom for sourcing sustainable seafood and a seasonal guide to produce. So, roll up your sleeves and let's get started!

Essential Ingredients of the Atlantic Diet

The Atlantic Diet is a celebration of the bounty that comes from both the land and sea. At its core, you'll find a rich tapestry of flavors, each ingredient telling its own story.

- **Seafood:** The crown jewels of the Atlantic, offering everything from sardines and mackerel to clams and oysters. These sea treasures are not just about taste; they're packed with omega-3 fatty acids, essential for heart and brain health.
- **Fruits and Vegetables:** The vibrant colors of the market are your palette. Leafy greens, tomatoes, peppers, and a plethora of fruits like apples, pears, and citrus, form the foundation of many dishes, bringing vitamins, minerals, and fiber to your plate.
- **Whole Grains and Legumes:** From hearty bread to comforting bowls of beans, these staples provide the energy and sustenance that have fueled Atlantic communities for centuries.
- **Nuts and Seeds:** Almonds, walnuts, and chia seeds sprinkle dishes with crunch and nutrients, while olive oil reigns supreme as the preferred source of healthy fats, drizzled generously over dishes or used in cooking.
- **Herbs and Spices:** The Atlantic Diet is anything but bland, with herbs like parsley, cilantro, and bay leaves, alongside spices such as paprika and saffron, adding depth and complexity to every bite.

Tools and Equipment for the Atlantic Kitchen

A craftsman is only as good as their tools, and the same goes for the home chef. Here's what you'll need to bring the Atlantic Diet to life:

- **A Good Knife:** Every kitchen's workhorse, a sharp, reliable chef's knife will make prep work a breeze.
- **Cookware:** Invest in a sturdy skillet (cast iron is a fantastic choice), a large pot for stews and soups, and a baking dish for casseroles and roasts. A seafood steamer or a paella pan can also be wonderful additions.
- **Miscellaneous:** Don't forget a cutting board, mixing bowls, a colander, and basic utensils like spatulas, tongs, and a whisk. A mortar and pestle for grinding fresh herbs and spices can elevate your dishes to the next level.

Tips for Sourcing Sustainable Seafood

In an age where the health of our oceans is more important than ever, choosing sustainable seafood is crucial. Here's how you can make responsible choices:

- **Look for Labels:** Certifications like the Marine Stewardship Council (MSC) or the Aquaculture Stewardship Council (ASC) indicate sustainable practices.
- **Ask Questions:** Don't hesitate to ask your fishmonger about the origin of their seafood and the methods used to catch or farm it. Transparency is key.
- **Go Local:** Whenever possible, choose local and seasonal seafood. Not only does it support local economies, but it also reduces your carbon footprint.
- **Diversify Your Choices:** Opt for less popular species to avoid putting pressure on overfished populations. This not only helps the ecosystem but also introduces you to new flavors.

A Guide to Seasonal Produce in the Atlantic Region

Eating seasonally is at the heart of the Atlantic Diet, not just for the freshest flavors but also for the joy of connecting with the rhythm of nature. Here's a brief guide to get you started:

- **Spring:** As the earth awakens, look for tender greens like spinach and arugula, artichokes, and the first strawberries of the year. It's a time for renewal, both in nature and on your plate.
- **Summer:** The abundance of summer brings tomatoes, peppers, cucumbers, and a variety of fruits like peaches, cherries, and melons. Seafood is also plentiful, making it perfect for outdoor grills and family picnics.
- **Fall:** The harvest season offers a bounty of root vegetables, squash, and late berries. It's also the time for hearty greens like kale and the first of the season's apples and pears.
- **Winter:** While the landscape may seem barren, the ocean still provides. Look for robust vegetables like cabbages and potatoes, citrus fruits, and hardy fish species. It's a season for warming stews and comforting bakes.

Through these essentials, you're now equipped to navigate the rich and nourishing path of the Atlantic Diet. Each ingredient, tool, and piece of knowledge brings you closer to mastering the art of Atlantic cooking, transforming your kitchen into a haven of health and flavor. Remember, the journey is as important as the destination, so embrace each step, experiment with new ingredients, and above all, enjoy the process of creating dishes that not only feed the body but also nourish the soul. Welcome to the Atlantic Kitchen—your adventure starts here.

Chapter 1: Starters and Snacks

Welcome to the delightful world of traditional seafood tapas, where the ocean's bounty meets the joy of sharing. These ten easy recipes are your ticket to hosting memorable get-togethers or simply enjoying a taste of the Atlantic Diet any day of the week. Let's dive in!

1. Classic Garlic Shrimp (Gambas al Ajillo)

INGREDIENTS:
- 1 lb large shrimp, peeled and deveined
- 6 cloves garlic, thinly sliced
- ½ cup olive oil
- 1 tsp red pepper flakes
- Salt to taste
- Fresh parsley, chopped (for garnish)
- 1 lemon, wedged (for serving)

PREP TIME: 10 minutes

Method:

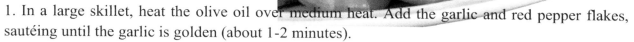

1. In a large skillet, heat the olive oil over medium heat. Add the garlic and red pepper flakes, sautéing until the garlic is golden (about 1-2 minutes).
2. Increase the heat to high and add the shrimp. Cook, stirring frequently, until the shrimp are pink and cooked through (about 3-4 minutes).
3. Season with salt, garnish with parsley, and serve immediately with lemon wedges on the side. Enjoy this sizzling dish straight from the skillet!

2. Marinated Mussels (Mejillones en Escabeche)

INGREDIENTS:
- 2 lbs fresh mussels, cleaned
- 1 cup white wine
- ½ cup olive oil
- ¼ cup white wine vinegar
- 1 bay leaf
- 3 cloves garlic, minced
- 1 tsp paprika
- Salt and pepper to taste
- Fresh parsley, chopped (for garnish)

PREP TIME: 20 minutes

Method:

1. In a large pot, combine the mussels and white wine. Cover and steam over medium heat until the mussels open (about 5-7 minutes). Discard any that do not open.

2. Remove the mussels from the shell and place them in a bowl. In another bowl, whisk together olive oil, vinegar, bay leaf, garlic, paprika, salt, and pepper.

3. Pour the marinade over the mussels, ensuring they are well coated. Refrigerate for at least 2 hours or overnight.

4. Serve chilled, garnished with fresh parsley. These marinated mussels are a refreshing and tangy treat!

3. Crispy Squid Rings (Calamares a la Romana)

INGREDIENTS:
- 1 lb squid, cleaned and cut into rings
- 1 cup all-purpose flour
- 2 eggs, beaten
- Salt and pepper to taste
- Olive oil for frying
- Lemon wedges (for serving)

PREP TIME: 15 minutes

Method:
1. Season the squid rings with salt and pepper. Dredge in flour, dip in beaten eggs, and then coat again in flour.

2. Heat a good amount of olive oil in a deep skillet over medium-high heat. Fry the squid rings in batches until golden and crispy (about 2-3 minutes per side).

3. Drain on paper towels and serve hot with lemon wedges. These crispy squid rings are a crunchy delight!

4. Anchovy-Stuffed Olives (Aceitunas Rellenas de Anchoa)

INGREDIENTS:
- 1 cup large green olives, pitted
- 12 anchovy fillets
- ½ cup olive oil
- 2 cloves garlic, minced
- 1 tsp red pepper flakes

PREP TIME: 10 minutes

Method:
1. Carefully stuff each olive with an anchovy fillet. Set aside.

2. In a small bowl, mix together olive oil, garlic, and red pepper flakes.

3. Pour the olive oil mixture over the stuffed olives, ensuring they are well coated.

4. Let marinate for at least 1 hour before serving. These bite-sized snacks pack a flavorful punch!

5. Tuna-Stuffed Piquillo Peppers (Pimientos del Piquillo Rellenos de Atún)

INGREDIENTS:
- 1 cup canned tuna, drained
- ½ cup mayonnaise
- 1 tbsp capers, chopped
- Salt and pepper to taste
- 12 piquillo peppers, drained

PREP TIME: 15 minutes

Method:
1. In a bowl, mix together the tuna, mayonnaise, capers, salt, and pepper until well combined.
2. Carefully stuff each piquillo pepper with the tuna mixture.
3. Serve chilled or at room temperature. These stuffed peppers are a simple yet elegant appetizer.

6. Clam and Chorizo Bites (Almejas con Chorizo)

INGREDIENTS:
- 1 lb small clams, cleaned
- ½ lb chorizo, diced
- 1 onion, finely chopped
- 2 cloves garlic, minced
- ½ cup white wine
- Fresh parsley, chopped (for garnish)

PREP TIME: 20 minutes

Method:
1. In a large pan, cook the chorizo over medium heat until crispy. Remove and set aside, leaving the oils in the pan.
2. In the same pan, add the onion and garlic, sautéing until soft. Add the clams and white wine, cover, and steam until the clams open (about 5-7 minutes).
3. Add the chorizo back to the pan, mix well, and cook for an additional 2 minutes.
4. Serve hot, garnished with fresh parsley. The combination of clams and chorizo is irresistible!

7. Garlic Mushroom Caps (Champiñones al Ajillo)

INGREDIENTS:
- 1 lb large mushrooms, stems removed

- 6 cloves garlic, minced
- ½ cup olive oil
- 2 tbsp lemon juice
- Salt and pepper to taste
- Fresh parsley, chopped (for garnish)

PREP TIME: 10 minutes

Method:

1. In a large skillet, heat the olive oil over medium heat. Add the garlic and cook until fragrant (about 1 minute).

2. Add the mushroom caps, gill-side up, and cook for 5 minutes. Flip and cook for another 5 minutes, or until tender.

3. Drizzle with lemon juice, season with salt and pepper, and garnish with parsley before serving. These garlic mushrooms are a juicy and flavorful treat!

8. Cod Croquettes (Croquetas de Bacalao)

INGREDIENTS:
- 1 lb cod fillet, cooked and flaked
- 2 cups milk
- 4 tbsp butter
- ½ cup all-purpose flour, plus extra for coating
- 2 eggs, beaten
- Bread crumbs for coating
- Olive oil for frying
- Salt and pepper to taste

PREP TIME: 30 minutes (plus chilling)

Method:

1. In a saucepan, melt the butter over medium heat. Add ½ cup flour and cook for 2 minutes, stirring constantly.

2. Gradually add the milk, whisking continuously until the mixture thickens. Stir in the flaked cod, season with salt and pepper, and cook for an additional 2 minutes.

3. Transfer the mixture to a dish and chill in the refrigerator for at least 2 hours.

4. Once chilled, shape the mixture into small croquettes. Coat each croquette in flour, dip in beaten eggs, and then roll in breadcrumbs.

5. Fry the croquettes in hot olive oil until golden and crispy. Drain on paper towels and serve hot. These cod croquettes are a crunchy outside, tender inside marvel!

9. Octopus and Potato Salad (Ensalada de Pulpo y Patata)

INGREDIENTS:
- 1 lb octopus, cooked and sliced
- 2 lbs potatoes, boiled and cubed
- ½ cup olive oil
- 2 tbsp lemon juice
- 1 tsp paprika
- Salt and pepper to taste
- Fresh parsley, chopped (for garnish)

PREP TIME: 20 minutes

Method:
1. In a large bowl, combine the octopus and potatoes.
2. In a small bowl, whisk together olive oil, lemon juice, paprika, salt, and pepper.
3. Pour the dressing over the octopus and potatoes, tossing gently to coat.
4. Serve chilled or at room temperature, garnished with fresh parsley. This salad is a refreshing blend of sea and earth flavors!

10. Sardine Pâté on Toast (Paté de Sardinas en Tostada)

INGREDIENTS:
- 1 can sardines in olive oil, drained
- 1 tbsp mayonnaise
- 1 tsp lemon juice
- 1 clove garlic, minced
- Salt and pepper to taste
- Toasted baguette slices

PREP TIME: 10 minutes

Method:
1. In a bowl, mash the sardines with a fork. Mix in mayonnaise, lemon juice, garlic, salt, and pepper until well combined.
2. Spread the sardine pâté generously on toasted baguette slices.
3. Serve immediately for a quick, flavorful bite. This sardine pâté is a simple yet sophisticated way to start any meal!

Seasonal Vegetables Antipasti

1. Roasted Asparagus with Lemon Zest

INGREDIENTS:
- 1 bunch of fresh asparagus, trimmed
- 2 tablespoons olive oil
- Zest of 1 lemon
- Salt and pepper to taste

PREP TIME: 10 minutes

Method:
1. Preheat your oven to 400°F (200°C).
2. Toss the asparagus in olive oil, lemon zest, salt, and pepper.
3. Spread them out on a baking sheet in a single layer.
4. Roast for 15-20 minutes, until tender but still crisp.
5. Serve warm or at room temperature.

2. Cherry Tomato and Basil Skewers

INGREDIENTS:
- 1 pint cherry tomatoes
- Fresh basil leaves
- Mozzarella balls
- Balsamic glaze
- Salt and pepper to taste

PREP TIME: 15 minutes

Method:
1. Thread cherry tomatoes, basil leaves, and mozzarella balls onto small skewers.
2. Drizzle with balsamic glaze and sprinkle with salt and pepper.
3. Serve immediately or refrigerate until serving.

3. Grilled Zucchini Ribbons

INGREDIENTS:
- 2 zucchinis, sliced into thin ribbons
- 2 tablespoons olive oil
- Salt and pepper to taste
- Lemon wedges, for serving

PREP TIME: 10 minutes

Method:

1. Preheat your grill to medium-high.
2. Toss zucchini ribbons with olive oil, salt, and pepper.
3. Grill for about 2 minutes on each side, until charred and tender.
4. Serve with lemon wedges on the side.

4. Marinated Bell Peppers

INGREDIENTS:

- 3 bell peppers (red, yellow, green), sliced
- ¼ cup olive oil
- 2 tablespoons red wine vinegar
- 1 garlic clove, minced
- Salt and pepper to taste
- Fresh parsley, chopped

PREP TIME: 15 minutes + Marinating

Method:

1. Grill or roast the bell peppers until charred, then place them in a bowl covered with plastic wrap for 10 minutes.
2. Peel the skins off the peppers and slice.
3. Whisk together olive oil, vinegar, garlic, salt, and pepper.
4. Toss the peppers in the marinade and let sit for at least 1 hour.
5. Sprinkle with fresh parsley before serving.

5. Cucumber and Dill Bites

INGREDIENTS:

- 1 large cucumber, sliced into rounds
- Cream cheese, softened
- Fresh dill, chopped
- Salt and pepper to taste

PREP TIME: 10 minutes

Method:

1. Spread each cucumber round with cream cheese.
2. Sprinkle with dill, salt, and pepper.
3. Arrange on a platter and serve chilled.

6. Stuffed Mini Peppers

INGREDIENTS:
- 12 mini bell peppers, halved and seeded
- 1 cup cooked quinoa
- ½ cup feta cheese, crumbled
- ¼ cup olives, chopped
- 2 tablespoons olive oil
- Salt and pepper to taste

PREP TIME: 20 minutes

Method:
1. Preheat your oven to 350°F (175°C).
2. Mix quinoa, feta, olives, olive oil, salt, and pepper in a bowl.
3. Stuff each pepper half with the mixture.
4. Bake for 15-20 minutes, until peppers are tender.
5. Serve warm or at room temperature.

7. Beetroot Carpaccio

INGREDIENTS:
- 2 large beetroots, peeled and thinly sliced
- 2 tablespoons olive oil
- 1 tablespoon balsamic vinegar
- Salt and pepper to taste
- Goat cheese, crumbled
- Walnuts, chopped

PREP TIME: 15 minutes

Method:
1. Arrange beetroot slices on a platter.
2. Whisk together olive oil, balsamic vinegar, salt, and pepper.
3. Drizzle the dressing over the beetroots.
4. Sprinkle with goat cheese and walnuts before serving.

8. Eggplant Rolls with Ricotta

INGREDIENTS:
- 1 eggplant, sliced lengthwise
- 1 cup ricotta cheese
- Fresh basil, chopped
- Salt and pepper to taste

- Olive oil, for grilling

PREP TIME: 20 minutes

Method:

1. Grill eggplant slices brushed with olive oil until tender.
2. Mix ricotta with basil, salt, and pepper.
3. Place a spoonful of the mixture on each eggplant slice and roll up.
4. Serve at room temperature or chilled.

9. Radish and Butter Crostini

INGREDIENTS:

- Baguette, sliced and toasted
- Softened butter
- Radishes, thinly sliced
- Sea salt and fresh black pepper

PREP TIME: 10 minutes

Method:

1. Spread each baguette slice with butter.
2. Top with radish slices, then sprinkle with sea salt and pepper.
3. Serve immediately for a crunchy, buttery bite.

10. Carrot and Hummus Tartlets

INGREDIENTS:

- Mini tart shells, prebaked
- Hummus
- Carrots, shredded
- Paprika
- Fresh parsley, for garnish

PREP TIME: 15 minutes

Method:

1. Fill each tart shell with a spoonful of hummus.
2. Top with shredded carrots and a sprinkle of paprika.
3. Garnish with fresh parsley.
4. Chill until serving.

Atlantic Diet Dips and Spreads.

1. Classic Hummus with Atlantic Twist

INGREDIENTS:
- 1 can chickpeas, drained and rinsed
- 2 tablespoons tahini
- 1 garlic clove, minced
- 2 tablespoons olive oil
- Juice of 1 lemon
- A pinch of sea salt
- 1 teaspoon smoked paprika

PREP TIME: 10 minutes

Method:
1. In a food processor, blend chickpeas, tahini, garlic, olive oil, and lemon juice until smooth.
2. Season with sea salt and blend again.
3. Transfer to a serving dish and sprinkle with smoked paprika. Drizzle a bit more olive oil on top for that luscious finish.

2. Avocado & Yogurt Sea Dip

INGREDIENTS:
- 1 ripe avocado, peeled and pitted
- 1/2 cup Greek yogurt
- Juice of 1 lime
- 1 tablespoon chopped cilantro
- Salt and pepper to taste

PREP TIME: 5 minutes

Method:
1. Mash the avocado in a bowl using a fork.
2. Stir in Greek yogurt, lime juice, and cilantro until well combined.
3. Season with salt and pepper. Voilà, creamy and dreamy!

3. Sardine Pâté

INGREDIENTS:
- 1 can sardines in olive oil, drained
- 1 tablespoon cream cheese

- 1 teaspoon Dijon mustard
- Juice of 1/2 lemon
- A pinch of black pepper

PREP TIME: 5 minutes

Method:

1. In a bowl, mash the sardines with a fork.
2. Mix in cream cheese, Dijon mustard, lemon juice, and black pepper until smooth.
3. Serve with a dash of elegance and a sprinkle of chopped parsley if you're feeling fancy.

4. Roasted Red Pepper Spread

INGREDIENTS:

- 2 roasted red peppers, peeled and seeded
- 1 garlic clove
- 1/4 cup toasted almonds
- 2 tablespoons olive oil
- Salt to taste

PREP TIME: 10 minutes (plus roasting time if starting with fresh peppers)

Method:

1. Blend roasted red peppers, garlic, almonds, and olive oil in a food processor until smooth.
2. Season with salt. There you have it, a spread that's as vibrant in color as it is in flavor!

5. Tzatziki with a Crunch

INGREDIENTS:

- 1 cup Greek yogurt
- 1 small cucumber, finely diced
- 2 tablespoons chopped dill
- 1 garlic clove, minced
- Juice of 1/2 lemon
- Salt and pepper to taste

PREP TIME: 10 minutes

Method:

1. Combine Greek yogurt, cucumber, dill, garlic, and lemon juice in a bowl.
2. Season with salt and pepper, give it a good mix, and chill. Refreshing, right?

6. Mackerel & Horseradish Cream

INGREDIENTS:

- 1 can mackerel, drained

- 2 tablespoons cream cheese
- 1 teaspoon prepared horseradish
- 1 tablespoon chopped chives
- A squeeze of lemon juice

PREP TIME: 5 minutes

Method:

1. Mash mackerel in a bowl.
2. Stir in cream cheese, horseradish, chives, and lemon juice until well combined.
3. Taste and think of the sea!

7. Olive Tapenade

INGREDIENTS:
- 1 cup pitted Kalamata olives
- 2 tablespoons capers, rinsed
- 1 garlic clove
- 2 tablespoons olive oil
- Juice of 1/2 lemon

PREP TIME: 10 minutes

Method:

1. Pulse olives, capers, and garlic in a food processor until coarsely chopped.
2. With the motor running, slowly add olive oil and lemon juice.
3. Spread on toast and feel the Mediterranean vibes.

8. White Bean & Herb Spread

INGREDIENTS:
- 1 can white beans, drained and rinsed
- 2 tablespoons olive oil
- 1 tablespoon chopped rosemary
- 1 garlic clove, minced
- Salt and pepper to taste

PREP TIME: 5 minutes

Method:

1. Blend white beans, olive oil, rosemary, and garlic until smooth.
2. Season with salt and pepper. Simple, healthy, and utterly delicious.

9. Spicy Pumpkin Seed Dip

INGREDIENTS:

- 1 cup toasted pumpkin seeds
- 1 jalapeño, seeded and chopped
- 1/4 cup cilantro leaves
- 2 tablespoons lime juice
- 1/4 cup olive oil
- Salt to taste

PREP TIME: 10 minutes

Method:

1. In a food processor, blend pumpkin seeds, jalapeño, cilantro, and lime juice.
2. Gradually add olive oil until smooth.
3. Season with salt. Dive into this unique, nutty, and slightly spicy dip.

10. Carrot & Ginger Puree

INGREDIENTS:
- 2 carrots, cooked and softened
- 1 inch piece of ginger, grated
- 2 tablespoons olive oil
- Salt and pepper to taste

PREP TIME: 5 minutes (excluding cooking time for carrots)

Method:

1. Puree cooked carrots and grated ginger in a blender.
2. While blending, slowly add olive oil until you reach a smooth consistency.
3. Season with salt and pepper. It's sweet, it's spicy, it's everything nice!

And there you have it, ten easy and delightful dips and spreads to bring a taste of the Atlantic into your home. Whether you're looking for something creamy, crunchy, or with a bit of zing, there's something here for every palate. Enjoy experimenting, and don't forget to share the joy with friends and family!

Chapter 2: Soups and Salads

Hearty Fish Stews and Broths

Dive into the comforting embrace of the ocean with these 10 hearty fish stew and broth recipes. Simple yet bursting with flavor, these dishes are a testament to the Atlantic Diet's versatility and its dedication to bringing the sea's bounty straight to your table. Let's get cooking, shall we?

1. Classic Fisherman's Stew

INGREDIENTS:
- 1 lb mixed seafood (shrimp, mussels, and firm white fish like cod)
- 1 onion, chopped
- 2 garlic cloves, minced
- 1 can diced tomatoes
- 2 cups fish or vegetable broth
- 1 teaspoon dried oregano
- 2 tablespoons olive oil
- Salt and pepper to taste
- Chopped parsley for garnish

PREP TIME: 20 minutes

Method:
1. In a large pot, heat olive oil over medium heat. Add onion and garlic, sautéing until soft.
2. Pour in the diced tomatoes, broth, and oregano, bringing to a simmer.
3. Add the seafood, cover, and cook for about 5 minutes or until the fish is cooked through and the mussels have opened.
4. Season with salt and pepper, garnish with parsley, and there you have a stew worthy of any seaside tavern.

2. Simple Cod and Potato Broth

INGREDIENTS:
- 2 large potatoes, cubed
- 1 lb cod fillets, cut into chunks
- 1 onion, chopped
- 2 carrots, sliced
- 4 cups vegetable broth

- 2 tablespoons olive oil
- Salt and pepper to taste
- Fresh dill for garnish

PREP TIME: 30 minutes

Method:

1. Heat olive oil in a pot. Add onion and carrots, cooking until they start to soften.
2. Add the potatoes and broth, bringing to a boil. Reduce heat and simmer until potatoes are nearly tender.
3. Add the cod chunks, simmering gently until the fish flakes easily.
4. Season to taste, garnish with dill, and enjoy this heartwarming broth.

3. Spicy Shrimp and Tomato Stew

INGREDIENTS:

- 1 lb shrimp, peeled and deveined
- 1 can diced tomatoes
- 1 onion, diced
- 2 garlic cloves, minced
- 1 jalapeño, seeded and chopped
- 2 cups fish broth
- 1 teaspoon paprika
- 2 tablespoons olive oil
- Salt to taste
- Cilantro for garnish

PREP TIME: 25 minutes

Method:

1. In a pot, heat the olive oil over medium. Sauté onion, garlic, and jalapeño until onion is translucent.
2. Stir in the diced tomatoes, fish broth, and paprika, simmering for about 10 minutes.
3. Add the shrimp, cooking until they turn pink and are cooked through.
4. Season with salt, garnish with cilantro, and serve this spicy delight with a side of crusty bread.

4. Hearty Salmon Chowder

INGREDIENTS:

- 1 lb salmon fillet, cubed
- 2 cups potatoes, cubed
- 1 cup corn (fresh or frozen)
- 1 onion, chopped
- 2 cups milk

- 2 cups vegetable broth
- 2 tablespoons butter
- Salt and pepper to taste
- Fresh chives for garnish

PREP TIME: 30 minutes

Method:

1. In a large pot, melt the butter and cook the onion until soft.
2. Add potatoes and broth, bringing to a boil before lowering the heat to simmer until potatoes are tender.
3. Stir in the salmon, corn, and milk, cooking gently until the salmon is cooked through.
4. Season with salt and pepper, garnish with chives, and let every spoonful warm you up.

5. Mediterranean Mussels Soup

INGREDIENTS:
- 2 lbs mussels, cleaned and debearded
- 1 can diced tomatoes
- 1 onion, chopped
- 3 garlic cloves, minced
- 1/2 cup white wine
- 2 cups fish broth
- 2 tablespoons olive oil
- 1 teaspoon dried thyme
- Salt and pepper to taste
- Chopped parsley for garnish

PREP TIME: 20 minutes

Method:

1. In a large pot, heat the olive oil and sauté the onion and garlic until soft.
2. Add white wine, letting it simmer for a few minutes to reduce slightly.
3. Stir in the diced tomatoes, fish broth, and thyme, bringing to a gentle simmer.
4. Add the mussels, cover, and cook until they open up, about 5 to 8 minutes.
5. Season with salt and pepper, garnish with parsley, and dive into this Mediterranean marvel.

6. Creamy Haddock Soup

INGREDIENTS:
- 1 lb haddock fillet, cut into pieces
- 2 potatoes, cubed
- 1 leek, sliced
- 2 cups milk

- 2 cups fish broth
- 2 tablespoons butter
- Salt and pepper to taste
- Dill for garnish

PREP TIME: 35 minutes

Method:

1. In a pot, melt butter over medium heat. Add leeks, cooking until soft but not browned.
2. Add potatoes and fish broth, simmering until potatoes are tender.
3. Gently add the haddock and milk, simmering until the fish is cooked through.
4. Season with salt and pepper, garnish with dill, and revel in the creamy goodness.

7. Tomato and Sea Bass Stew

INGREDIENTS:
- 1 lb sea bass fillets, cut into chunks
- 1 can diced tomatoes
- 1 onion, diced
- 2 garlic cloves, minced
- 2 cups vegetable broth
- 1 teaspoon dried basil
- 2 tablespoons olive oil
- Salt and pepper to taste
- Basil leaves for garnish

PREP TIME: 25 minutes

Method:

1. Heat olive oil in a pot. Add onion and garlic, sautéing until translucent.
2. Stir in diced tomatoes, vegetable broth, and dried basil, simmering for about 10 minutes to let the flavors meld.
3. Add sea bass chunks, cooking gently until they're just done.
4. Season with salt and pepper, garnish with fresh basil, and serve this stew with a sense of seaside sophistication.

8. Clam and Corn Broth

INGREDIENTS:
- 2 cans clams in juice
- 1 cup corn (fresh or frozen)
- 1 potato, diced
- 1 onion, chopped
- 2 cups vegetable broth

- 1 cup heavy cream
- 2 tablespoons butter
- Salt and pepper to taste
- Chopped parsley for garnish

PREP TIME: 30 minutes

Method:

1. In a pot, melt the butter and cook the onion until soft.
2. Add potato and broth, simmering until the potato is tender.
3. Stir in clams with their juice, corn, and heavy cream, heating through without letting it boil.
4. Season with salt and pepper, garnish with parsley, and enjoy a bowl full of comfort.

9. Easy Peasy Fish Soup

INGREDIENTS:
- 1 lb firm white fish (like tilapia), cubed
- 1 can diced tomatoes
- 1 onion, diced
- 2 carrots, sliced
- 2 cups fish broth
- 1 teaspoon dried dill
- 2 tablespoons olive oil
- Salt and pepper to taste
- Lemon wedges for serving

PREP TIME: 25 minutes

Method:

1. In a large pot, heat the olive oil and sauté the onion and carrots until tender.
2. Add the diced tomatoes, fish broth, and dill, bringing to a simmer.
3. Add the fish cubes, simmering gently until they're cooked through.
4. Season with salt and pepper, serve with a squeeze of lemon, and bask in its simplicity and flavor.

10. Spicy Cod Soup

INGREDIENTS:
- 1 lb cod fillets, cut into chunks
- 1 can diced tomatoes with chilies
- 1 onion, chopped
- 2 garlic cloves, minced
- 2 cups fish broth
- 1 teaspoon cumin
- 2 tablespoons olive oil

- Salt to taste
- Fresh cilantro for garnish
PREP TIME: 25 minutes
Method:
1. Heat olive oil in a pot. Add onion and garlic, cooking until they begin to soften.
2. Stir in the diced tomatoes with chilies, fish broth, and cumin, simmering for about 10 minutes.
3. Add the cod chunks, cooking gently until they flake easily.
4. Season with salt, garnish with cilantro, and let this soup's warmth and spice take you on a delightful journey.

There you go— comforting, easy-to-make fish stews and broths that bring the essence of the Atlantic Diet right into your kitchen. Whether you're craving something creamy, spicy, or brimming with the ocean's bounty, these recipes are sure to satisfy. Happy cooking, and may each bowl bring you closer to the sea's heart!

Fresh and Crisp Atlantic Salads

Welcome to the refreshing world of salads where the crispness of the produce meets the tang of the dressing, creating a symphony of flavors and textures. These 10 Atlantic-inspired salads are not just about greens; they're a celebration of the ocean's bounty and the earth's harvest. So, let's get chopping and tossing!

1. Atlantic Seabreeze Salad

INGREDIENTS:
- Mixed greens (arugula, spinach, and romaine)
- 1 avocado, sliced
- 1/2 cucumber, thinly sliced
- 1/4 cup red onions, thinly sliced
- 1/2 cup cherry tomatoes, halved
- 1/4 cup feta cheese, crumbled
- 2 tablespoons olive oil
- Juice of 1 lemon
- Salt and pepper to taste
PREP TIME: 10 minutes
Method:
1. In a large bowl, toss the mixed greens, avocado, cucumber, red onions, and cherry tomatoes.
2. Drizzle with olive oil and lemon juice, then season with salt and pepper.
3. Sprinkle feta cheese on top. There you have it—a salad as refreshing as a sea breeze!

2. Citrusy Seafood Salad

INGREDIENTS:
- 1 cup cooked shrimp, peeled
- 1 orange, segmented
- 1 grapefruit, segmented
- Mixed greens of your choice
- 1/4 cup sliced almonds
- 2 tablespoons olive oil
- 1 tablespoon white wine vinegar
- Salt and pepper to taste

PREP TIME: 15 minutes

Method:

1. Arrange mixed greens on a plate. Top with shrimp, orange segments, and grapefruit segments.
2. In a small bowl, whisk together olive oil, white wine vinegar, salt, and pepper.
3. Drizzle the dressing over the salad and sprinkle with sliced almonds. Dive into this citrusy delight!

3. Rustic Tuna & Bean Salad

INGREDIENTS:
- 1 can tuna in olive oil, drained
- 1 can white beans, drained and rinsed
- 1 red onion, thinly sliced
- 2 tablespoons capers
- 2 tablespoons parsley, chopped
- 3 tablespoons olive oil
- Juice of 1 lemon
- Salt and pepper to taste

PREP TIME: 10 minutes

Method:

1. In a bowl, mix tuna, white beans, red onion, capers, and parsley.
2. Dress with olive oil and lemon juice, then season with salt and pepper.
3. Toss everything together for a rustic, hearty salad that's brimming with flavors.

4. Sardine and Roasted Pepper Salad

INGREDIENTS:
- 1 can sardines in olive oil, drained
- 1 cup roasted red peppers, sliced

- 1/4 cup black olives, pitted and sliced
- Mixed greens
- 2 tablespoons olive oil
- 1 tablespoon balsamic vinegar
- Salt and pepper to taste

PREP TIME: 10 minutes

Method:

1. Lay a bed of mixed greens on a plate.
2. Arrange sardines, roasted red peppers, and black olives on top.
3. Whisk together olive oil, balsamic vinegar, salt, and pepper, and drizzle over the salad. It's a simple yet bold salad that packs a punch!

5. Apple and Walnut Ocean Salad

INGREDIENTS:
- Mixed greens
- 1 apple, thinly sliced
- 1/2 cup walnuts, toasted and chopped
- 1/4 cup blue cheese, crumbled
- 2 tablespoons olive oil
- 1 tablespoon cider vinegar
- Salt and pepper to taste

PREP TIME: 10 minutes

Method:

1. Combine mixed greens, apple slices, and walnuts in a bowl.
2. In a separate bowl, whisk together olive oil, cider vinegar, salt, and pepper.
3. Drizzle the dressing over the salad, then top with blue cheese. It's a crisp, sweet, and tangy salad that's absolutely irresistible.

6. Beetroot and Goat Cheese Seaside Salad

INGREDIENTS:
- 2 beetroots, cooked and sliced
- Mixed greens
- 1/4 cup goat cheese, crumbled
- 2 tablespoons sunflower seeds
- 2 tablespoons olive oil
- 1 tablespoon balsamic glaze
- Salt and pepper to taste

PREP TIME: 10 minutes

Method:

1. Arrange mixed greens on a plate, and top with sliced beetroots.

2. Sprinkle goat cheese and sunflower seeds over the top.

3. Drizzle with olive oil and balsamic glaze, then season with salt and pepper. A salad that's as beautiful as it is delicious.

7. Cucumber and Yogurt Atlantic Salad

INGREDIENTS:

- 2 cucumbers, diced
- 1/2 cup Greek yogurt
- 2 tablespoons dill, chopped
- 1 garlic clove, minced
- Juice of 1/2 lemon
- Salt and pepper to taste

PREP TIME: 10 minutes

Method:

1. In a bowl, mix cucumbers, Greek yogurt, dill, garlic, and lemon juice.

2. Season with salt and pepper and give it a good stir. It's refreshing, creamy, and perfect for a light meal or side dish.

8. Quinoa and Avocado Shoreline Salad

INGREDIENTS:

- 1 cup cooked quinoa
- 1 avocado, diced
- 1/2 cup cherry tomatoes, halved
- 1/4 cup corn kernels, cooked
- 1/4 cup cilantro, chopped
- 2 tablespoons lime juice
- 2 tablespoons olive oil
- Salt and pepper to taste

PREP TIME: 15 minutes

Method:

1. In a large bowl, combine quinoa, avocado, cherry tomatoes, corn, and cilantro.

2. Dress with lime juice and olive oil, then season with salt and pepper.

3. Toss everything together for a salad that's as nutritious as it is flavorful.

9. Seaweed and Sesame Salad

INGREDIENTS:
- 1 cup dried seaweed, rehydrated
- 1 cucumber, thinly sliced
- 2 tablespoons sesame seeds, toasted
- 2 tablespoons soy sauce
- 1 tablespoon sesame oil
- 1 tablespoon rice vinegar

PREP TIME: 15 minutes (including seaweed rehydration)

Method:

1. Mix rehydrated seaweed and cucumber slices in a bowl.

2. In a small bowl, whisk together sesame seeds, soy sauce, sesame oil, and rice vinegar.

3. Pour the dressing over the seaweed and cucumber, tossing well to coat. It's a crunchy, umami-packed salad that will transport you straight to the coast.

10. Lobster and Mango Salad

INGREDIENTS:
- 1 cup cooked lobster meat, chopped
- 1 mango, diced
- 1 avocado, diced
- 1/4 cup red onion, finely chopped
- Mixed greens
- 2 tablespoons olive oil
- 1 tablespoon lime juice
- Salt and chili flakes to taste

PREP TIME: 20 minutes

Method:

1. In a bowl, mix lobster meat, mango, avocado, and red onion.

2. Lay a bed of mixed greens on a serving plate.

3. Top with the lobster mixture. Whisk together olive oil, lime juice, salt, and chili flakes, and drizzle over the salad. A luxurious salad that's sure to impress.

Warm Grain and Legume Salads

Ready to cozy up with some hearty warmth? These warm grain and legume salads are like a hug in a bowl! Perfect for those chilly evenings or when you just need something satisfying. Let's get into the kitchen and whip up some comforting goodness.

1. Warm Quinoa and Black Bean Salad

INGREDIENTS:
- 1 cup quinoa
- 1 can black beans, drained and rinsed
- 1 red bell pepper, diced
- 1 cup corn (frozen or fresh)
- 1/2 red onion, finely chopped
- 2 tablespoons lime juice
- 1/4 cup chopped cilantro
- Salt and pepper to taste
- 2 tablespoons olive oil

PREP TIME: 20 minutes

Method:
1. Cook quinoa according to package instructions. Fluff with a fork and set aside to cool slightly.
2. In a large bowl, mix warm quinoa with black beans, red bell pepper, corn, and red onion.
3. Dress with lime juice, olive oil, and season with salt and pepper.
4. Toss in chopped cilantro before serving. Simple, yet so full of flavor!

2. Warm Lentil and Roasted Vegetable Salad

INGREDIENTS:
- 1 cup green lentils
- 2 carrots, diced
- 1 sweet potato, diced
- 1 red onion, quartered
- 3 tablespoons olive oil
- 2 tablespoons balsamic vinegar
- Salt and pepper to taste
- 1/4 cup crumbled feta cheese (optional)

PREP TIME: 40 minutes

Method:
1. Cook lentils according to package instructions. Drain and set aside.
2. Toss carrots, sweet potato, and red onion with 2 tablespoons olive oil and roast in a preheated oven at 425°F for 25 minutes.
3. Whisk together remaining olive oil and balsamic vinegar for the dressing.
4. Mix warm lentils and roasted vegetables. Drizzle with dressing, season with salt and pepper, and sprinkle feta cheese on top. It's a rainbow on your plate!

3. Warm Barley and Mushroom Salad

INGREDIENTS:
- 1 cup pearl barley
- 2 cups mushrooms, sliced
- 1 garlic clove, minced
- 4 tablespoons olive oil, divided
- 2 tablespoons soy sauce
- 1/4 cup parsley, chopped
- Salt and pepper to taste

PREP TIME: 30 minutes

Method:

1. Cook barley according to package instructions. Set aside to cool slightly.

2. Sauté mushrooms and garlic in 2 tablespoons of olive oil until golden. Season with a little salt and pepper.

3. Toss warm barley with sautéed mushrooms, adding soy sauce and remaining olive oil

4. Finish with a sprinkle of fresh parsley. Earthy and utterly comforting!

4. Warm Farro, Spinach, and Chickpea Salad

INGREDIENTS:
- 1 cup farro
- 1 can chickpeas, drained and rinsed
- 3 cups baby spinach
- 1/2 lemon, zest and juice
- 1/4 cup grated Parmesan cheese
- 3 tablespoons olive oil
- Salt and pepper to taste

PREP TIME: 30 minutes

Method:

1. Cook farro according to package instructions. Drain and transfer to a large mixing bowl.

2. While farro is still warm, add chickpeas and baby spinach. The heat will slightly wilt the spinach.

3. Add lemon zest, lemon juice, olive oil, and season with salt and pepper.

4. Toss everything together and garnish with Parmesan cheese. A delightful blend of textures and flavors!

5. Warm Bulgur, Beet, and Orange Salad

INGREDIENTS:
- 1 cup bulgur

- 2 medium beets, roasted and diced
- 1 orange, segmented
- 1/4 cup walnuts, toasted and chopped
- 2 tablespoons olive oil
- 1 tablespoon red wine vinegar
- Salt and pepper to taste
- A handful of arugula for serving

PREP TIME: 45 minutes (including roasting beets)

Method:

1. Cook bulgur according to package instructions. Fluff and set aside to cool slightly.

2. In a large bowl, combine warm bulgur, diced beets, and orange segments.

3. Dress with olive oil and red wine vinegar. Season with salt and pepper.

4. Serve on a bed of arugula and sprinkle with toasted walnuts. The perfect sweet and earthy combo!

6. Warm Sorghum Salad with Roasted Cauliflower

INGREDIENTS:
- 1 cup sorghum
- 2 cups cauliflower florets
- 2 tablespoons olive oil, divided
- 1 teaspoon curry powder
- 1/4 cup dried cranberries
- 1/4 cup slivered almonds, toasted
- Salt and pepper to taste

PREP TIME: 50 minutes

Method:

1. Cook sorghum according to package instructions. Set aside.

2. Toss cauliflower florets with 1 tablespoon olive oil and curry powder. Roast at 425°F for 20-25 minutes until tender and golden.

3. Mix warm sorghum with roasted cauliflower, dried cranberries, and slivered almonds.

4. Dress with remaining olive oil, season with salt and pepper, and serve. A delightful crunch with every bite!

7. Warm Millet, Pomegranate, and Kale Salad

INGREDIENTS:
- 1 cup millet
- 2 cups kale, chopped
- 1/2 cup pomegranate seeds

- 1/4 cup pumpkin seeds, toasted
- 2 tablespoons apple cider vinegar
- 3 tablespoons olive oil
- Salt and pepper to taste

PREP TIME: 25 minutes

Method:

1. Cook millet according to package instructions. Fluff and let cool slightly.

2. In a large bowl, massage kale with a bit of olive oil until slightly wilted.

3. Add warm millet, pomegranate seeds, and pumpkin seeds to the kale.

4. Dress with apple cider vinegar and olive oil. Season with salt and pepper. This salad is not only beautiful but bursting with flavors!

8. Warm Brown Rice and Edamame Salad

INGREDIENTS:
- 1 cup brown rice
- 1 cup edamame, shelled and cooked
- 1 red bell pepper, diced
- 2 scallions, thinly sliced
- 2 tablespoons sesame oil
- 1 tablespoon soy sauce
- 1 teaspoon honey
- Sesame seeds for garnish

PREP TIME: 30 minutes

Method:

1. Cook brown rice according to package instructions. Let cool slightly.

2. In a large bowl, mix warm brown rice, edamame, red bell pepper, and scallions.

3. Whisk together sesame oil, soy sauce, and honey for the dressing.

4. Toss the salad with the dressing, sprinkle with sesame seeds, and serve. A touch of Asia in every spoonful!

9. Warm Couscous, Tomato, and Zucchini Salad

INGREDIENTS:
- 1 cup couscous
- 1 zucchini, diced
- 1 cup cherry tomatoes, halved
- 1/4 cup kalamata olives, pitted and sliced
- 2 tablespoons olive oil
- Juice of 1 lemon

- Salt and pepper to taste
- Feta cheese for garnish

PREP TIME: 20 minutes

Method:

1. Prepare couscous according to package instructions. Fluff and let cool slightly.

2. Sauté zucchini in 1 tablespoon olive oil until just tender. Cool slightly.

3. In a large bowl, combine couscous, sautéed zucchini, cherry tomatoes, and kalamata olives.

4. Dress with lemon juice and remaining olive oil. Season with salt and pepper.

5. Garnish with crumbled feta cheese before serving. Fresh, quick, and utterly satisfying!

10. Warm Chickpea and Sweet Potato Salad

INGREDIENTS:
- 1 can chickpeas, drained and rinsed
- 1 large sweet potato, diced and roasted
- 2 tablespoons olive oil, divided
- 1 teaspoon smoked paprika
- 1/4 cup parsley, chopped
- 2 tablespoons tahini
- Juice of 1 lemon
- Salt and pepper to taste

PREP TIME: 35 minutes

Method:

1. Preheat oven to 425°F. Toss diced sweet potato with 1 tablespoon olive oil and smoked paprika. Roast for 20-25 minutes until tender.

2. In a large bowl, mix warm chickpeas and roasted sweet potato.

3. Whisk together tahini, lemon juice, and remaining olive oil to create the dressing.

4. Pour dressing over salad, add chopped parsley, and season with salt and pepper. Stir to combine. Every bite is a little bit of heaven!

There you go, ten warm grain and legume salads that are perfect for any day. They're easy to make, packed with nutrients, and absolutely delicious. Enjoy the warmth and comfort they bring!

Chapter 3: Main Courses

Ah, the main event! There's something truly special about sitting down to a beautifully prepared dish, especially when it features the bounty of the sea. Let's dive into the heart of Atlantic cuisine with 10 signature seafood dishes that are as easy to make as they are delicious. Whether you're a seasoned chef or just starting out, these recipes are sure to impress.

1. Simple Grilled Sardines

INGREDIENTS:
- 1 lb fresh sardines, cleaned and gutted
- 2 tbsp olive oil
- Salt and pepper to taste
- 1 lemon, sliced for serving
- Fresh parsley, chopped for garnish

PREP TIME: 10 minutes

Cook Time: 6 minutes

Method:
1. Preheat your grill to medium-high heat.
2. Toss sardines in olive oil, salt, and pepper.
3. Grill sardines for 3 minutes on each side or until the skin is crispy and the fish flakes easily.
4. Serve hot with a squeeze of lemon and a sprinkle of fresh parsley.

2. Garlic Shrimp Tapas

INGREDIENTS:
- 1 lb shrimp, peeled and deveined
- 4 cloves garlic, thinly sliced
- 1/4 cup olive oil
- 1 tsp red pepper flakes
- Salt to taste
- 2 tbsp fresh parsley, chopped
- Lemon wedges for serving

PREP TIME: 15 minutes

Cook Time: 6 minutes

Method:
1. In a large skillet, heat olive oil over medium heat.
2. Add garlic and red pepper flakes, sautéing until fragrant.

3. Increase the heat to high, add shrimp and salt, and cook for 2-3 minutes on each side until pink and cooked through.

4. Garnish with parsley and serve with lemon wedges on the side.

3. Baked Cod with Lemon and Herbs

INGREDIENTS:
- 4 cod fillets
- 2 tbsp olive oil
- Salt and pepper to taste
- 1 lemon, thinly sliced
- 2 tbsp fresh dill, chopped
- 2 tbsp fresh parsley, chopped

PREP TIME: 10 minutes

Cook Time: 12-15 minutes

Method:

1. Preheat oven to 400°F (200°C).

2. Place cod fillets in a baking dish. Drizzle with olive oil and season with salt and pepper.

3. Top each fillet with lemon slices and sprinkle with dill and parsley.

4. Bake in the preheated oven for 12-15 minutes, or until the fish flakes easily with a fork.

4. Pan-Seared Scallops with Butter Sauce

INGREDIENTS:
- 1 lb sea scallops, side muscle removed
- Salt and pepper to taste
- 2 tbsp olive oil
- 2 tbsp unsalted butter
- 1 garlic clove, minced
- Juice of 1 lemon
- 1 tbsp fresh parsley, chopped

PREP TIME: 10 minutes

Cook Time: 6 minutes

Method:

1. Pat scallops dry and season with salt and pepper.

2. Heat olive oil in a large skillet over high heat. Add scallops, searing for about 2-3 minutes on each side until a golden crust forms.

3. Lower the heat to medium, add butter and garlic to the skillet, cooking for 1 minute.

4. Squeeze lemon over scallops and garnish with parsley before serving.

5. Easy Mussels in White Wine Sauce

INGREDIENTS:
- 2 lbs mussels, cleaned and debearded
- 1 tbsp olive oil
- 4 cloves garlic, minced
- 1 cup dry white wine
- 2 tbsp unsalted butter
- 1/4 cup fresh parsley, chopped
- Crusty bread for serving

PREP TIME: 15 minutes

Cook Time: 10 minutes

Method:

1. In a large pot, heat olive oil over medium heat. Add garlic and sauté until fragrant.
2. Pour in white wine and bring to a simmer.
3. Add mussels, cover the pot, and cook for about 5-7 minutes until mussels have opened. Discard any that do not open.
4. Stir in butter and parsley, then serve hot with crusty bread to soak up the sauce.

6. Clam Linguine

INGREDIENTS:
- 1 lb linguine
- 2 tbsp olive oil
- 4 cloves garlic, minced
- 1 lb clams, cleaned
- 1/2 cup dry white wine
- 1/2 cup clam juice (or seafood broth)
- 2 tbsp fresh parsley, chopped
- Lemon wedges for serving

PREP TIME: 20 minutes

Cook Time: 15 minutes

Method:

1. Cook linguine according to package instructions; drain and set aside.
2. In a large skillet, heat olive oil over medium heat. Add garlic and sauté until golden.
3. Add clams, white wine, and clam juice. Cover and simmer for about 7-10 minutes until clams open.
4. Toss the cooked linguine with the clam sauce. Garnish with parsley and serve with lemon wedges.

7. Grilled Oysters with Garlic Butter

INGREDIENTS:
-12 large oysters, shucked, on the half shell
- 4 tbsp unsalted butter, melted
- 2 cloves garlic, minced
- 1 tbsp fresh parsley, chopped
- 1 tsp lemon zest
- Lemon wedges for serving
PREP TIME: 15 minutes
Cook Time: 5 minutes
Method:
1. Preheat your grill to high heat.
2. In a small bowl, mix melted butter with garlic, parsley, and lemon zest.
3. Place oysters on the grill, flat-side up. Spoon a bit of the garlic butter mixture onto each oyster.
4. Grill for about 5 minutes, or until the edges of the oysters start to curl slightly.
5. Serve immediately with lemon wedges on the side.

8. Simple Fish Tacos

INGREDIENTS:
- 1 lb white fish fillets (e.g., tilapia, cod)
- 2 tbsp olive oil
- 1 tsp chili powder
- 1 tsp cumin
- Salt and pepper to taste
- 8 small corn tortillas
- Fresh cabbage, thinly sliced
- Avocado, sliced
- Fresh cilantro, chopped
- Lime wedges for serving
PREP TIME: 20 minutes
Cook Time: 10 minute
Method:
1. Preheat your grill or skillet over medium-high heat.
2. Season fish fillets with olive oil, chili powder, cumin, salt, and pepper.
3. Cook fish for about 4-5 minutes on each side, until opaque and flaky.
4. Warm tortillas on the grill or in a skillet.
5. Break the fish into pieces and divide among tortillas. Top with cabbage, avocado, and cilantro.
6. Serve with lime wedges on the side.

9. Lobster Roll

INGREDIENTS:
- 4 lobster tails, steamed and chopped
- 2 tbsp mayonnaise
- 1 tbsp lemon juice
- 2 tbsp celery, finely chopped
- 2 tbsp fresh chives, chopped
- Salt and pepper to taste
- 4 hot dog buns, toasted
- Butter for buns

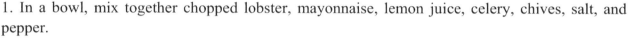

PREP TIME: 30 minutes
Cook Time: 10 minutes
Method:
1. In a bowl, mix together chopped lobster, mayonnaise, lemon juice, celery, chives, salt, and pepper.
2. Butter the insides of the hot dog buns and toast them until golden.
3. Fill each bun with the lobster mixture.
4. Serve immediately, perhaps with a side of crisp potato chips or a fresh salad.

10. Baked Haddock with Parmesan Crust

INGREDIENTS:
- 4 haddock fillets
- 2 tbsp olive oil
- Salt and pepper to taste
- 1/2 cup grated Parmesan cheese
- 1/4 cup breadcrumbs
- 1 tbsp Italian seasoning
- Lemon wedges for serving

PREP TIME: 10 minutes
Cook Time: 15 minutes
Method:
1. Preheat oven to 425°F (220°C).
2. Place haddock fillets in a baking dish. Drizzle with olive oil and season with salt and pepper.
3. In a small bowl, mix Parmesan cheese, breadcrumbs, and Italian seasoning. Sprinkle this mixture over the haddock fillets.
4. Bake in the preheated oven for 15 minutes, or until the crust is golden and the fish flakes easily with a fork.
5. Serve hot with lemon wedges on the side.

Vegetarian Delights of the Atlantic Coast

Embarking on a vegetarian journey along the Atlantic Coast brings a kaleidoscope of flavors, colors, and textures. These dishes are a testament to the region's rich bounty, proving that vegetarian cuisine is anything but boring. Let's dive into ten easy yet utterly delightful recipes that will make your taste buds dance with joy.

1. Atlantic Seaside Gazpacho

INGREDIENTS:
- 4 ripe tomatoes, chopped
- 1 cucumber, peeled and chopped
- 1 green bell pepper, chopped
- 1 small red onion, chopped
- 2 cloves garlic, minced
- 3 tbsp olive oil
- 2 tbsp sherry vinegar
- Salt and pepper to taste
- Ice-cold water (optional, for desired consistency)

PREP TIME: 15 minutes + chilling

Method:

1. Combine tomatoes, cucumber, bell pepper, onion, and garlic in a blender. Blitz until smooth.

2. Add olive oil and sherry vinegar. Blitz again. Season with salt and pepper.

3. For a thinner consistency, add a little ice-cold water and blend again.

4. Chill for at least an hour. Serve cold with a drizzle of olive oil and a sprinkle of chopped cucumber and bell pepper on top.

2. Roasted Veggie and Quinoa Salad

INGREDIENTS:
- 1 cup quinoa, rinsed
- 2 cups vegetable broth
- 1 zucchini, sliced
- 1 red bell pepper, chopped
- 1 eggplant, chopped
- 2 tbsp olive oil
- Salt and pepper to taste
- 2 tbsp lemon juice
- 1/4 cup feta cheese, crumbled (optional)

- Fresh parsley, chopped (for garnish)

PREP TIME: 30 minutes

Method:

1. Preheat your oven to 400°F (200°C).

2. Toss zucchini, bell pepper, and eggplant with olive oil, salt, and pepper. Roast for 20 minutes, or until tender.

3. Meanwhile, cook quinoa in vegetable broth according to package instructions.

4. Combine roasted veggies, cooked quinoa, and lemon juice in a large bowl. Adjust seasoning.

5. Garnish with feta (if using) and fresh parsley before serving.

3. Atlantic Coast Potato and Leek Soup

INGREDIENTS:
- 3 leeks, cleaned and sliced
- 2 lbs potatoes, peeled and diced
- 4 cups vegetable broth
- 2 tbsp olive oil
- Salt and pepper to taste
- Chives, chopped (for garnish)

PREP TIME: 45 minutes

Method:

1. Heat olive oil in a large pot over medium heat. Add leeks and cook until softened.

2. Add potatoes and vegetable broth. Bring to a boil, then simmer until potatoes are tender.

3. Use an immersion blender to purée the soup until smooth. Season with salt and pepper.

4. Serve hot, garnished with chopped chives.

4. Chickpea and Spinach Stew

INGREDIENTS:
- 2 cans chickpeas, drained and rinsed
- 4 cups fresh spinach, washed
- 1 onion, diced
- 2 cloves garlic, minced
- 1 can diced tomatoes
- 1 tsp smoked paprika
- 2 tbsp olive oil
- Salt and pepper to taste

PREP TIME: 30 minutes

Method:

1. Heat olive oil in a pot over medium heat. Sauté onion and garlic until translucent.

2. Add chickpeas, diced tomatoes, and smoked paprika. Cook for 10 minutes.

3. Add spinach and cook until wilted. Season with salt and pepper.

4. Serve warm, perhaps with crusty bread on the side.

5. Baked Atlantic Herb Frittata

INGREDIENTS:
- 8 eggs
- 1/2 cup milk
- 1 zucchini, sliced
- 1 red bell pepper, diced
- 1/2 cup grated cheese (your choice)
- 2 tbsp mixed fresh herbs (e.g., parsley, chives, thyme)
- Salt and pepper to taste
- 1 tbsp olive oil

PREP TIME: 35 minutes

Method:
1. Preheat your oven to 375°F (190°C).

2. Whisk together eggs, milk, salt, and pepper.

3. Heat olive oil in an oven-safe skillet over medium heat. Sauté zucchini and bell pepper until just soft.

4. Pour egg mixture over the veggies. Sprinkle with cheese and herbs.

5. Bake for 20-25 minutes, or until the frittata is set and lightly golden.

6. Serve warm, cut into wedges.

6. Simple Lentil Salad with Mustard Vinaigrette

INGREDIENTS:
- 2 cups cooked lentils (green or brown)
- 1 cucumber, diced
- 1 tomato, diced
- 1/4 cup red onion, finely chopped
- 2 tbsp olive oil
- 1 tbsp Dijon mustard
- 2 tbsp apple cider vinegar
- Salt and pepper to taste
- Fresh parsley, chopped (for garnish)

PREP TIME: 20 minutes

Method:
1. In a large bowl, combine cooked lentils, cucumber, tomato, and red onion.

2. In a small bowl, whisk together olive oil, Dijon mustard, apple cider vinegar, salt, and pepper to create the vinaigrette.

3. Pour vinaigrette over the lentil mixture and toss to coat evenly.

4. Garnish with fresh parsley before serving. This salad can be enjoyed cold or at room temperature.

7. Stuffed Bell Peppers with Rice and Vegetables

INGREDIENTS:
- 4 bell peppers, tops cut off and seeds removed
- 1 cup cooked rice
- 1 zucchini, finely diced
- 1 carrot, finely diced
- 1/2 cup corn kernels
- 1 onion, diced
- 2 cloves garlic, minced
- 1 can diced tomatoes
- 1 tsp dried oregano
- 1/2 cup shredded cheese (optional)
- 2 tbsp olive oil
- Salt and pepper to taste

PREP TIME: 1 hour

Method:
1. Preheat your oven to 350°F (175°C).
2. Heat olive oil in a pan over medium heat. Sauté onion, garlic, zucchini, and carrot until soft.
3. Stir in cooked rice, corn, diced tomatoes, oregano, salt, and pepper. Cook for another 5 minutes.
4. Fill each bell pepper with the rice and vegetable mixture. Top with cheese if desired.
5. Place stuffed peppers in a baking dish with a little water at the bottom. Cover with foil.
6. Bake for 45 minutes, or until the peppers are tender. Remove foil in the last 10 minutes to brown the tops.

8. Creamy Atlantic Pumpkin Soup

INGREDIENTS:
- 2 lbs pumpkin, peeled and cubed
- 1 onion, diced
- 2 cloves garlic, minced
- 4 cups vegetable broth
- 1 cup coconut milk
- 2 tbsp olive oil

- 1 tsp ground nutmeg
- Salt and pepper to taste
- Pumpkin seeds (for garnish)

PREP TIME: 50 minutes

Method:

1. Heat olive oil in a large pot over medium heat. Sauté onion and garlic until translucent.

2. Add pumpkin cubes and cook for 5 minutes. Pour in vegetable broth and bring to a boil.

3. Reduce heat and simmer until the pumpkin is tender. Blend the soup until smooth using an immersion blender.

4. Stir in coconut milk and nutmeg. Season with salt and pepper.

5. Serve hot, garnished with pumpkin seeds.

9. Atlantic Mushroom Risotto

INGREDIENTS:
- 1 cup Arborio rice
- 3 cups vegetable broth, warmed
- 2 cups mixed mushrooms, sliced (e.g., shiitake, cremini, portobello)
- 1 onion, finely chopped
- 2 cloves garlic, minced
- 1/2 cup white wine (optional)
- 1/4 cup grated Parmesan cheese (optional)
- 2 tbsp olive oil
- Salt and pepper to taste
- Fresh parsley, chopped (for garnish)

PREP TIME: 45 minutes

Method:

1. Heat 1 tablespoon of olive oil in a large pan over medium heat. Add mushrooms and cook until browned. Set aside.

2. In the same pan, add another tablespoon of olive oil. Sauté onion and garlic until soft.

3. Add Arborio rice and stir for 2 minutes until the grains are well-coated and slightly translucent.

4. Pour in the white wine (if using) and stir until absorbed.

5. Add vegetable broth, one ladle at a time, stirring continuously until the liquid is absorbed before adding the next ladle. This process should take about 20-25 minutes, or until the rice is creamy and just tender.

6. Stir in the cooked mushrooms, season with salt and pepper, and add Parmesan cheese if desired.

7. Serve garnished with fresh parsley.

10. Quinoa Stuffed Acorn Squash

INGREDIENTS:
- 2 acorn squash, halved and seeds removed
- 1 cup quinoa, cooked
- 1 apple, diced
- 1/4 cup dried cranberries
- 1/4 cup walnuts, chopped
- 1/2 tsp cinnamon
- 2 tbsp maple syrup
- 2 tbsp olive oil
- Salt and pepper to taste

PREP TIME: 1 hour

Method:

1. Preheat your oven to 375°F (190°C). Brush acorn squash halves with olive oil and season with salt and pepper.
2. Place squash halves cut-side down on a baking sheet. Roast for about 25-30 minutes, or until tender.
3. In a bowl, mix cooked quinoa, apple, dried cranberries, walnuts, cinnamon, and maple syrup.
4. Once the squash is roasted, flip them over and fill with the quinoa mixture.
5. Return to the oven and bake for an additional 20 minutes.
6. Serve warm, drizzled with a little more maple syrup if desired.

Meat and Poultry with Atlantic Flavors

Diving into the heart of our cookbook, the main courses are where the Atlantic Diet truly shines. Let's explore some meat and poultry dishes that encapsulate the essence of the Atlantic, each bursting with flavor and surprisingly easy to make. Get ready to impress not just your taste buds but your loved ones too!

1. Simple Atlantic Herb-Roasted Chicken

INGREDIENTS:
- 1 whole chicken (about 4-5 lbs)
- 2 tbsp olive oil
- 1 lemon, halved
- 4 garlic cloves, minced
- 1 tbsp fresh rosemary, chopped
- 1 tbsp fresh thyme, chopped

- Salt and pepper to taste
PREP TIME: 15 minutes
Cook Time: 1 hour 20 minutes
Method:
1. Preheat your oven to 375°F (190°C).
2. In a small bowl, mix olive oil, garlic, rosemary, thyme, salt, and pepper.
3. Rub the chicken inside and out with the herb mixture. Place lemon halves inside the cavity.
4. Roast in the oven until the skin is golden and a thermometer inserted into the thickest part reads 165°F (74°C). Let it rest before carving.

2. Pan-Seared Pork Chops with Apple Cider Glaze

INGREDIENTS:
- 4 pork chops, bone-in
- Salt and pepper to taste
- 2 tbsp olive oil
- 1 cup apple cider
- 2 tsp Dijon mustard
- 1 apple, thinly sliced
- 1 small onion, sliced
PREP TIME: 10 minutes
Cook Time: 25 minutes
Method:
1. Season pork chops with salt and pepper.
2. Heat oil in a skillet over medium-high heat. Add pork chops and sear until golden, about 5 minutes per side. Remove and set aside.
3. In the same skillet, add apple cider, mustard, apple, and onion. Cook until the sauce thickens and apples are tender.
4. Return pork chops to the skillet and coat with the glaze. Cook until pork chops are done.

3. Atlantic Salmon Wrapped in Prosciutto

INGREDIENTS:
- 4 salmon fillets
- 8 slices of prosciutto
- 1 tbsp olive oil
- 1 lemon, for serving
- Fresh dill, for garnish
- Salt and pepper to taste
PREP TIME: 10 minutes

Cook Time: 15 minutes

Method:

1. Preheat your oven to 400°F (200°C).

2. Season salmon fillets with salt and pepper. Wrap each fillet with 2 slices of prosciutto.

3. Heat oil in an ovenproof skillet over medium-high heat. Add salmon and sear each side for 2 minutes.

4. Transfer the skillet to the oven and bake for about 10 minutes, or until salmon is cooked through.

5. Serve with a squeeze of lemon and garnish with fresh dill.

4. Garlic and Herb Lamb Chops

INGREDIENTS:

- 8 lamb chops
- 2 tbsp olive oil
- 3 garlic cloves, minced
- 1 tbsp fresh rosemary, chopped
- 1 tbsp fresh thyme, chopped
- Salt and pepper to taste

PREP TIME: 10 minutes

Cook Time: 10 minutes

Method:

1. Season lamb chops with salt, pepper, garlic, rosemary, and thyme.

2. Heat oil in a skillet over medium-high heat. Add lamb chops and cook for about 3-4 minutes on each side for medium-rare.

3. Let them rest for a few minutes before serving to let the juices redistribute.

5. Beef Tenderloin with Port Wine Reduction

INGREDIENTS:

- 1 beef tenderloin (about 2 lbs)
- Salt and pepper to taste
- 2 tbsp olive oil
- 1 cup port wine
- 2 shallots, minced
- 1 cup beef broth
- 2 tbsp butter

PREP TIME: 15 minutes

Cook Time: 35 minutes

Method:

1. Preheat your oven to 400°F (200°C).

2. Season the beef tenderloin with salt and pepper.

3. Heat oil in an ovenproof skillet over medium-high heat. Sear the tenderloin on all sides until golden.

4. Transfer to the oven and roast for about 25 minutes for medium-rare. Remove and let it rest.

5. In the same skillet, add shallots and cook until soft. Deglaze with port wine, add beef broth, and reduce by half. Whisk in butter until glossy.

6. Slice the tenderloin and serve with the port wine reduction.

6. Quick Atlantic Spiced Meatballs

INGREDIENTS:
- 1 lb ground beef
- 1 egg, beaten
- 1/4 cup breadcrumbs
- 2 garlic cloves, minced
- 1 tsp paprika
- 1 tsp cumin
- Salt and pepper to taste
- 2 tbsp olive oil
- 1 can (14 oz) diced tomatoes

PREP TIME: 15 minutes

Cook Time: 20 minutes

Method:

1. In a bowl, mix ground beef, egg, breadcrumbs, garlic, paprika, cumin, salt, and pepper until well combined.

2. Form into small meatballs.

3. Heat oil in a skillet over medium heat. Add meatballs and cook until browned on all sides.

4. Add diced tomatoes and simmer until the sauce thickens and meatballs are cooked through.

7. Atlantic-Style Roasted Turkey Breast

INGREDIENTS:
- 1 turkey breast (about 3 lbs)
- 2 tbsp olive oil
- 2 tsp thyme, chopped
- 2 tsp rosemary, chopped
- 3 garlic cloves, minced
- Salt and pepper to taste

PREP TIME: 10 minutes

Cook Time: 1 hour

Method:

1. Preheat your oven to 350°F (175°C).

2. In a small bowl, mix olive oil, thyme, rosemary, garlic, salt, and pepper. Rub this mixture all over the turkey breast.

3. Place the turkey breast in a roasting pan and roast for about 1 hour, or until the internal temperature reaches 165°F (74°C).

4. Let it rest before slicing.

8. Grilled Duck Breast with Berry Sauce

INGREDIENTS:

- 2 duck breasts, skin scored
- Salt and pepper to taste
- 1 cup mixed berries (such as raspberries, blueberries, or blackberries)
- 1/4 cup balsamic vinegar
- 2 tbsp honey
- 1 tbsp butter

PREP TIME: 15 minutes

Cook Time: 20 minutes

Method:

1. Season duck breasts with salt and pepper.

2. Heat a grill pan over medium-high heat. Place duck breasts skin-side down and cook until the skin is crisp, about 5-7 minutes. Flip and cook for another 5 minutes for medium-rare. Let rest.

3. In a saucepan, combine berries, balsamic vinegar, and honey. Cook until the berries break down and the sauce thickens. Stir in butter.

4. Slice duck breasts and serve with the berry sauce.

9. Easy Peasy Lemon Squeezy Chicken Skewers

INGREDIENTS:

- 2 lbs chicken breast, cut into chunks
- 2 lemons, juiced and zest
- 3 tbsp olive oil
- 2 garlic cloves, minced
- 1 tsp oregano
- Salt and pepper to taste
- Wooden skewers, soaked in water

PREP TIME: 20 minutes (plus marinating time)

Cook Time: 10 minutes

Method:

1. In a bowl, mix lemon juice and zest, olive oil, garlic, oregano, salt, and pepper. Add chicken chunks and marinate for at least 1 hour.
2. Thread the marinated chicken onto skewers.
3. Heat a grill or grill pan over medium-high heat. Grill skewers, turning occasionally, until chicken is cooked through.

10. Balsamic Glazed Pork Tenderloin

INGREDIENTS:
- 1 pork tenderloin (about 1 lb)
- Salt and pepper to taste
- 2 tbsp olive oil
- 1/4 cup balsamic vinegar
- 2 tbsp honey
- 1 garlic clove, minced

PREP TIME: 10 minutes

Cook Time: 25 minutes

Method:
1. Preheat your oven to 375°F (190°C).
2. Season the pork tenderloin with salt and pepper.
3. Heat oil in an ovenproof skillet over medium-high heat. Add the tenderloin and sear on all sides.
4. Mix balsamic vinegar, honey, and garlic in a bowl. Pour over the tenderloin.
5. Transfer the skillet to the oven and roast for about 15-20 minutes, basting occasionally with the glaze, until the internal temperature reaches 145°F (63°C).
6. Let it rest before slicing and serving with the glaze.

Each recipe is designed to bring a taste of the Atlantic into your home, no matter where you are. Enjoy cooking, and more importantly, enjoy eating!

Chapter 4: Sides and Accompaniments

Welcome to the vibrant world of seasonal vegetable sides! Whether you're looking to brighten up a winter's day or make the most of summer's bounty, these easy, delicious recipes are here to complement any meal with a splash of Atlantic flair. Let's dive into the garden's treasures, shall we?

1. Spring Pea and Mint Salad

INGREDIENTS: 2 cups fresh peas, 1/4 cup fresh mint (chopped), 2 tablespoons olive oil, 1 tablespoon lemon juice, salt, and pepper to taste.
PREP TIME: 10 minutes
- **Method:**
   1. Blanch peas in boiling water for 1-2 minutes, then plunge into ice water.
   2. Drain peas and mix with chopped mint.
   3. Whisk together olive oil and lemon juice, season with salt and pepper, and dress the peas. Serve chilled for a refreshing side.

2. Summer Grilled Zucchini

INGREDIENTS: 4 zucchinis (sliced lengthwise), 2 tablespoons olive oil, salt, and pepper, 1 teaspoon thyme.
PREP TIME: 15 minutes
- **Method:**
   1. Preheat your grill to medium-high heat.
   2. Toss zucchini slices in olive oil, salt, pepper, and thyme.
   3. Grill for 3-4 minutes on each side or until tender and charred. Serve warm for a smoky, savory side.

3. Autumn Roasted Root Vegetables

INGREDIENTS: 2 carrots, 2 parsnips, 1 small sweet potato, all peeled and chopped, 2 tablespoons olive oil, salt, and pepper, 1 teaspoon rosemary.
PREP TIME: 40 minutes
- **Method:**

1. Preheat oven to 400°F (200°C).
2. Toss vegetables with olive oil, salt, pepper, and rosemary.
3. Spread on a baking sheet and roast for 30 minutes, stirring halfway through. Enjoy the sweet, earthy flavors that taste like fall.

4. Winter Cabbage Slaw

INGREDIENTS: 1/2 head of red cabbage (thinly sliced), 2 carrots (julienned), 1/4 cup apple cider vinegar, 1 tablespoon honey, salt, and pepper.
PREP TIME: 15 minutes
- Method:
   1. Combine cabbage and carrots in a large bowl.
   2. In a small bowl, whisk together vinegar, honey, salt, and pepper.
   3. Pour dressing over vegetables and toss to coat. This crunchy, tangy slaw is a colorful pick-me-up during the colder months.

5. Garlic Green Beans

INGREDIENTS: 2 cups green beans (trimmed), 3 garlic cloves (minced), 1 tablespoon olive oil, salt, and pepper.
PREP TIME: 15 minutes
- Method:
   1. Blanch green beans in boiling water for 3 minutes, then plunge into ice water.
   2. Sauté garlic in olive oil until fragrant.
   3. Add green beans, season with salt and pepper, and cook for 2-3 minutes. Simple, garlicky goodness at its best!

6. Roasted Brussels Sprouts with Bacon

INGREDIENTS: 2 cups Brussels sprouts (halved), 4 slices of bacon (chopped), 1 tablespoon olive oil, salt, and pepper.
PREP TIME: 30 minutes
- Method:
   1. Preheat oven to 400°F (200°C).
   2. Toss Brussels sprouts with olive oil, salt, and pepper.
   3. Spread on a baking sheet and sprinkle with bacon.
   4. Roast for 20-25 minutes until crispy. A deliciously indulgent way to enjoy your greens!

7. Quick Pickled Radishes

INGREDIENTS: 1 bunch radishes (thinly sliced), 3/4 cup white vinegar, 1 tablespoon sugar, 2 teaspoons salt, 1 teaspoon mustard seeds.
PREP TIME: 10 minutes + chilling
- Method:
  1. Place radishes in a jar.
  2. Heat vinegar, sugar, salt, and mustard seeds until sugar dissolves.
  3. Pour over radishes and let chill. These zesty, crisp pickles add a punch to any plate.

8. Sauteed Spinach with Garlic

INGREDIENTS: 2 cups spinach, 2 garlic cloves (minced), 1 tablespoon olive oil, salt, and pepper.
PREP TIME: 10 minutes
- Method:
  1. Heat olive oil and sauté garlic until fragrant.
  2. Add spinach, season with salt and pepper, and cook until wilted. A quick, nutritious side that's packed with flavor.

9. Honey-Roasted Carrots

INGREDIENTS: 4 carrots (peeled and halved lengthwise), 2 tablespoons honey, 1 tablespoon olive oil, salt, and thyme.
PREP TIME: 35 minutes
- Method:
  1. Preheat oven to 400°F (200°C).
  2. Toss carrots with honey, olive oil, salt, and thyme.
  3. Roast for 30 minutes, turning once. Sweet, tender, and slightly caramelized, these carrots are irresistible.

10. Creamy Mashed Cauliflower

INGREDIENTS: 1 head of cauliflower (cut into florets), 1/4 cup milk, 2 tablespoons butter, salt, and pepper.
PREP TIME: 20 minutes
- Method:
  1. Steam cauliflower until very tender.
  2. Blend cauliflower with milk, butter, salt, and pepper until smooth. A lighter, creamier alternative to mashed potatoes that's just as comforting.

Whole Grains And Legumes

1. Simple Lemon-Parsley Quinoa

INGREDIENTS:
- 1 cup quinoa
- 2 cups water
- Zest and juice of 1 lemon
- 1/4 cup chopped fresh parsley
- Salt and pepper to taste
- 2 tablespoons olive oil

PREP TIME: 20 minutes

Method:
1. Rinse quinoa under cold water to remove its natural coating. This prevents bitterness.
2. In a saucepan, bring 2 cups of water to a boil. Add quinoa, cover, and simmer for about 15 minutes or until water is absorbed.
3. Remove from heat and let it sit, covered, for 5 minutes. Fluff with a fork.
4. Stir in lemon zest, lemon juice, parsley, olive oil, and season with salt and pepper. Serve warm or at room temperature.

2. Hearty Lentil Salad

INGREDIENTS:
- 1 cup green lentils
- 3 cups water
- 1 bay leaf (optional)
- 1/2 red onion, finely chopped
- 1 cucumber, diced
- 1 red bell pepper, diced
- 1/4 cup olive oil
- 2 tablespoons red wine vinegar
- Salt and pepper to taste
- Fresh parsley for garnish

PREP TIME: 30 minutes

Method:
1. Rinse lentils and combine with water and bay leaf in a pot. Bring to a boil, then simmer for 20-25 minutes until tender but not mushy. Drain and cool.
2. In a large bowl, mix the cooled lentils with onion, cucumber, and bell pepper.

3. Whisk together olive oil, vinegar, salt, and pepper. Pour over the lentil mixture and toss to coat.

4. Garnish with fresh parsley before serving. Enjoy this vibrant dish that's as nutritious as it is colorful!

3. Barley and Mushroom Pilaf

INGREDIENTS:
- 1 cup pearl barley
- 2.5 cups vegetable broth
- 1 cup mushrooms, sliced
- 1 onion, finely chopped
- 2 cloves garlic, minced
- 2 tablespoons olive oil
- Salt and pepper to taste
- Fresh thyme for garnish

PREP TIME: 40 minutes

Method:

1. Rinse barley under cold water.

2. In a pot, heat 1 tablespoon of olive oil over medium heat. Add onion and garlic, sautéing until translucent.

3. Add mushrooms and cook until they release their moisture and brown slightly.

4. Stir in barley, then add vegetable broth. Bring to a boil, reduce heat, cover, and simmer for about 30-35 minutes, or until barley is tender and liquid is absorbed.

5. Season with salt, pepper, and garnish with fresh thyme. This earthy and comforting pilaf is a hug in a bowl!

4. Simple Chickpea Salad

INGREDIENTS:
- 1 can (15 oz) chickpeas, drained and rinsed
- 1 cucumber, diced
- 1/2 red onion, finely chopped
- 1/2 cup cherry tomatoes, halved
- 1/4 cup fresh parsley, chopped
- 3 tablespoons olive oil
- 1 tablespoon lemon juice
- Salt and pepper to taste

PREP TIME: 10 minutes

Method:

1. In a large bowl, combine chickpeas, cucumber, onion, cherry tomatoes, and parsley.

2. Drizzle with olive oil and lemon juice, then season with salt and pepper.

3. Toss everything together until well mixed. Chill in the fridge for about 30 minutes before serving to let the flavors meld. This refreshing salad is your quick ticket to a nutritious side dish.

5. Warm Farro with Spinach and Cranberries

INGREDIENTS:
- 1 cup farro
- 3 cups water or vegetable broth
- 1 cup fresh spinach, roughly chopped
- 1/2 cup dried cranberries
- 1/4 cup walnuts, toasted and chopped
- 2 tablespoons olive oil
- Salt and pepper to taste
- A squeeze of lemon juice (optional)

PREP TIME: 30 minutes

Method:

1. Rinse farro under cold water. In a pot, bring water or broth to a boil, add farro, reduce heat to low, cover, and simmer for about 25-30 minutes, or until tender and chewy.

2. In the last few minutes of cooking, stir in spinach and let it wilt.

3. Remove from heat, stir in cranberries, walnuts, and olive oil. Season with salt, pepper, and a squeeze of lemon juice for an extra zing.

4. Serve warm as a hearty side dish that perfectly balances nutty farro, sweet cranberries, and earthy spinach. This dish is a testament to how simple ingredients can create a symphony of flavors.

6. Baked Sweet Potatoes with Black Bean Salsa

INGREDIENTS:
- 4 medium sweet potatoes, washed
- 1 can (15 oz) black beans, drained and rinsed
- 1 avocado, diced
- 1/2 red onion, finely chopped
- 1/2 cup corn kernels (fresh, frozen, or canned)
- 1/2 cup cherry tomatoes, quartered
- 1 lime, juiced
- 2 tablespoons olive oil
- Salt and pepper to taste
- Fresh cilantro for garnish

PREP TIME: 1 hour

Method:

1. Preheat your oven to 400°F (200°C). Prick sweet potatoes with a fork and bake directly on the oven rack for about 45-50 minutes, or until tender.

2. While the sweet potatoes are baking, prepare the salsa. In a bowl, combine black beans, avocado, red onion, corn, and cherry tomatoes. Add lime juice and olive oil. Season with salt and pepper and mix well.

3. Once sweet potatoes are done, let them cool slightly, then split them open and fluff the insides with a fork.

4. Top each sweet potato with a generous scoop of black bean salsa, garnish with fresh cilantro, and serve. These stuffed sweet potatoes offer a delightful mix of textures and tastes that are sure to please.

7. Quinoa and Beet Salad

INGREDIENTS:

- 1 cup quinoa
- 2 cups water
- 2 medium beets, roasted and diced
- 1/4 cup feta cheese, crumbled
- 1/4 cup walnuts, toasted and chopped
- 2 tablespoons olive oil
- 1 tablespoon balsamic vinegar
- Salt and pepper to taste
- Fresh parsley, chopped for garnish

PREP TIME: 45 minutes (includes roasting beets)

Method:

1. Rinse quinoa thoroughly under cold water. In a medium saucepan, combine quinoa and water. Bring to a boil, then cover and reduce heat to simmer for about 15 minutes, or until all water is absorbed.

2. Allow quinoa to cool, then transfer to a large bowl. Add the roasted beets, feta, and walnuts.

3. In a small bowl, whisk together olive oil and balsamic vinegar. Pour over the quinoa mixture and gently toss to combine.

4. Season with salt and pepper, garnish with fresh parsley, and serve. This salad is a beautiful blend of earthy beets, nutty quinoa, and the tangy bite of feta.

8. Mediterranean Bulgar Wheat Salad

INGREDIENTS:

- 1 cup bulgar wheat

- 2 cups boiling water
- 1 cucumber, diced
- 1/2 cup cherry tomatoes, halved
- 1/4 cup kalamata olives, pitted and halved
- 1/4 cup feta cheese, crumbled
- 1/4 cup fresh parsley, chopped
- 3 tablespoons olive oil
- 2 tablespoons lemon juice
- Salt and pepper to taste

PREP TIME: 20 minutes

Method:

1. Place bulgar in a large bowl. Pour boiling water over it, cover, and let stand for about 15 minutes, or until water is absorbed and bulgar is soft.

2. Fluff the bulgar with a fork and allow it to cool slightly. Add cucumber, cherry tomatoes, olives, and feta cheese to the bowl.

3. In a small bowl, whisk together olive oil and lemon juice. Pour over the salad and toss to combine.

4. Season with salt and pepper, sprinkle with fresh parsley, and serve. This light yet satisfying salad is perfect for a quick lunch or as a side dish.

9. Smoky Black Beans and Rice

INGREDIENTS:

- 1 cup long-grain white rice
- 2 cups water
- 1 can (15 oz) black beans, drained and rinsed
- 1 onion, finely chopped
- 2 cloves garlic, minced
- 1 teaspoon smoked paprika
- 2 tablespoons olive oil
- Salt and pepper to taste
- Fresh cilantro for garnish

PREP TIME: 30 minutes

Method:

1. In a saucepan, bring water to a boil. Add rice, reduce heat to low, cover, and simmer for 18-20 minutes, or until water is absorbed and rice is tender.

2. In another pan, heat olive oil over medium heat. Add onion and garlic, sautéing until soft and translucent.

3. Stir in black beans and smoked paprika, cooking until beans are heated through.

4. Serve the smoky black beans over the cooked rice, seasoned with salt and pepper, and garnished with fresh cilantro. This dish is a simple yet flavorful way to enjoy the classic combination of beans and rice.

10. Creamy Polenta with Roasted Vegetables

INGREDIENTS:
- 1 cup polenta (cornmeal)
- 4 cups water or vegetable broth
- 1 zucchini, sliced
- 1 red bell pepper, chopped
- 1 onion, sliced
- 1/4 cup Parmesan cheese, grated
- 2 tablespoons olive oil
- Salt and pepper to taste
- Fresh basil for garnish

PREP TIME: 40 minutes

Method:
1. Preheat oven to 400°F (200°C). Toss zucchini, bell pepper, and onion with 1 tablespoon olive oil, salt, and pepper. Spread on a baking sheet and roast for about 20 minutes, until vegetables are tender and lightly caramelized.
2. Meanwhile, in a large pot, bring water or broth to a boil. Gradually whisk in polenta, reduce heat to low, and cook, stirring frequently, until polenta is thick and creamy, about 15-20 minutes.
3. Stir in Parmesan cheese and the remaining olive oil into the polenta. Season with salt and pepper.
4. Serve the creamy polenta topped with roasted vegetables and garnished with fresh basil. This comforting dish beautifully showcases the creamy texture of polenta with the rich flavors of roasted vegetables.

Homemade Sauces and Dressings

1. Classic Olive Oil & Lemon Dressing

- **INGREDIENTS:**
  - ½ cup extra virgin olive oil
  - ¼ cup fresh lemon juice
  - 1 clove garlic, minced
  - Salt and pepper to taste

PREP TIME: 5 minutes

METHOD: In a small jar, combine all the ingredients. Seal the lid tightly and give it a good shake. Taste and adjust the seasoning if necessary. It's the perfect dressing for a simple green salad or drizzled over grilled vegetables.

2. Mediterranean Herb Vinaigrette

- **INGREDIENTS:**
  - ½ cup extra virgin olive oil
  - 3 tablespoons red wine vinegar
  - 1 teaspoon Dijon mustard
  - 1 teaspoon honey
  - 1 garlic clove, minced
  - 1 tablespoon mixed herbs (such as oregano, thyme, and basil), finely chopped
  - Salt and pepper to taste

PREP TIME: 5 minutes

METHOD: Whisk together all the ingredients in a bowl or shake them up in a jar. This vinaigrette brings a burst of Mediterranean flavors to any salad or roasted veggies.

3. Simple Garlic Aioli

- **INGREDIENTS:**
  - 1 cup mayonnaise
  - 2 cloves garlic, minced
  - 2 tablespoons lemon juice
  - Salt to taste

PREP TIME: 5 minutes

METHOD: Mix all the ingredients in a bowl until smooth. If you're feeling adventurous, add a sprinkle of paprika for a bit of warmth. Aioli is a fantastic dip for sweet potato fries or as a spread on sandwiches.

4. Tangy Yogurt & Dill Sauce

- **INGREDIENTS:**
  - 1 cup Greek yogurt
  - 2 tablespoons fresh dill, chopped
  - 1 clove garlic, minced
  - 2 tablespoons cucumber, finely diced
  - 1 tablespoon lemon juice
  - Salt and pepper to taste

PREP TIME: 10 minutes

METHOD: Combine all the ingredients in a bowl. Chill for an hour before serving to let the flavors meld. This sauce is a refreshing complement to grilled salmon or as a dressing for a cucumber salad.

5. Spicy Tomato Salsa

- **INGREDIENTS:**
  - 4 ripe tomatoes, diced
  - 1 small red onion, finely chopped
  - 1 jalapeño, seeded and finely chopped (adjust based on your heat preference)
  - ¼ cup fresh cilantro, chopped
  - Juice of 1 lime
  - Salt to taste

PREP TIME: 10 minutes

METHOD: Toss all the ingredients in a bowl. Let it sit for about 30 minutes to allow the flavors to combine. Serve with tortilla chips or as a topping for grilled fish tacos.

6. Creamy Avocado Dressing

- **INGREDIENTS:**
  - 1 ripe avocado
  - ½ cup Greek yogurt
  - 1 clove garlic, minced
  - 2 tablespoons lime juice
  - Salt and pepper to taste
  - Water (as needed to reach desired consistency)

PREP TIME: 5 minutes

METHOD: Blend all the ingredients until smooth, adding water a little at a time to get the consistency you like. It's delicious on a mixed green salad or as a dip for veggies.

7. Balsamic Reduction

- **INGREDIENTS:**
  - 1 cup balsamic vinegar

PREP TIME: 20 minutes

METHOD: Pour the vinegar into a small saucepan and bring to a boil. Reduce the heat and simmer until the vinegar has thickened and reduced by about half. Let it cool before drizzling over roasted Brussels sprouts or a caprese salad. It's magically sweet and tangy!

8. Fresh Basil Pesto

- **INGREDIENTS:**
  - 2 cups fresh basil leaves
  - ½ cup grated Parmesan cheese
  - ½ cup extra virgin olive oil
  - 1/3 cup pine nuts
  - 2 garlic cloves
  - Salt and pepper to taste

PREP TIME: 10 minutes

METHOD: Pulse all the ingredients in a food processor until smooth. Adjust the seasoning as needed. Pesto is versatile—mix it into pasta, spread on sandwiches, or dollop on top of soups.

9. Honey Mustard Dressing

- **INGREDIENTS:**
  - ¼ cup Dijon mustard
  - ¼ cup honey
  - ¼ cup apple cider vinegar
  - ¼ cup olive oil
  - Salt and pepper to taste

PREP TIME: 5 minutes

METHOD: Whisk together all the ingredients until well combined. It's a sweet and tangy dressing that pairs wonderfully with a crunchy cabbage slaw or as a dipping sauce for chicken tenders.

10. Chimichurri

- **INGREDIENTS:**
  - 1 cup fresh parsley, finely chopped
  - 3-4 cloves garlic, minced
  - 2 tablespoons fresh oregano leaves (or 2 teaspoons dried oregano)
  - ½ cup olive oil
  - 2 tablespoons red wine vinegar
  - 1 teaspoon red pepper flakes
  - Salt to taste

PREP TIME: 10 minutes

METHOD: Stir all the ingredients together in a bowl. Let it sit for at least 10 minutes to let the flavors meld together. Chimichurri is a vibrant addition to grilled steaks, chicken, or even roasted vegetables.

Each of these sauces and dressings brings its own unique flair to dishes, transforming simple ingredients into something extraordinary. Remember, cooking is all about experimenting and finding what tastes best to you, so don't be afraid to adjust these recipes to suit your palate. Happy cooking!

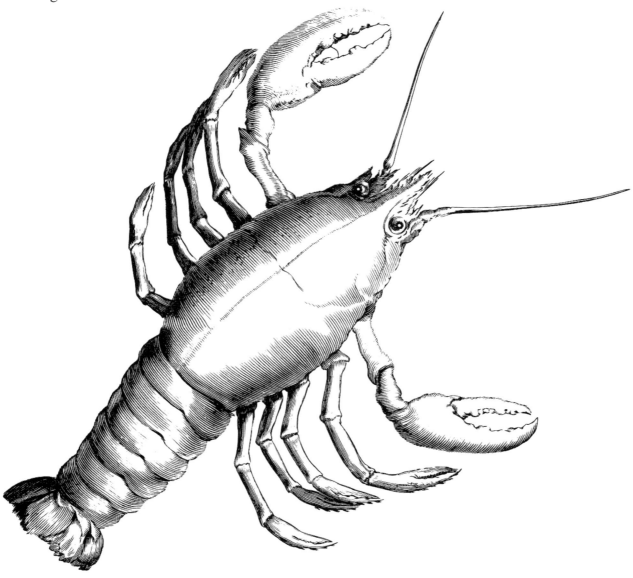

Chapter 5: Desserts

Welcome to the sweetest chapter of our Atlantic culinary adventure! In the spirit of the Atlantic Diet, we're keeping things light, fresh, and, most importantly, delicious. Desserts here are all about celebrating the natural sweetness and vibrant flavors of fruits, along with some indulgent yet healthy sweet treats and pastries. So, let's dive into these easy, mouth-watering recipes that will satisfy your sweet tooth without the guilt.

Fruit-Focused Desserts of the Atlantic

1. Berry and Yogurt Parfait

INGREDIENTS: Mixed berries (strawberries, blueberries, raspberries), Greek yogurt, honey, granola.
PREP TIME: 10 minutes.
METHOD: Layer Greek yogurt, a drizzle of honey, and mixed berries in a glass. Top with granola for a crunch.

2. Poached Pears in Red Wine

INGREDIENTS: 4 pears, 1 bottle red wine, 1 cup sugar, 2 cinnamon sticks, orange peel.
PREP TIME: 15 minutes + 1 hour cooking.
METHOD: Peel pears, leaving stems intact. In a pot, combine wine, sugar, cinnamon, and orange peel. Add pears; simmer until tender. Cool and serve.

3. Grilled Pineapple with Honey and Lime

INGREDIENTS: Pineapple slices, honey, lime zest, lime juice.
PREP TIME: 15 minutes.
METHOD: Grill pineapple slices until charred. Drizzle with honey and sprinkle lime zest and juice.

4. Apple Chips

INGREDIENTS: Apples, cinnamon.
PREP TIME: 10 minutes + 2 hours baking.

METHOD: Thinly slice apples, sprinkle with cinnamon, and bake at a low temp until crisp.

5. Berry Sorbet

INGREDIENTS: Frozen mixed berries, honey, lemon juice.
PREP TIME: 10 minutes + freezing.
METHOD: Blend berries, honey, and lemon juice until smooth. Freeze until set.

6. Citrus Salad with Mint

INGREDIENTS: Mixed citrus fruits (oranges, grapefruits, mandarins), honey, fresh mint.
PREP TIME: 15 minutes.
METHOD: Segment fruits, mix with a drizzle of honey, and garnish with mint.

7. Baked Figs with Goat Cheese

INGREDIENTS: Figs, goat cheese, honey, walnuts.
PREP TIME: 5 minutes + 15 minutes baking.
METHOD: Halve figs, top with goat cheese and walnuts, drizzle with honey, and bake.

8. Peach and Raspberry Crumble

INGREDIENTS: Peaches, raspberries, flour, oats, butter, sugar.
PREP TIME: 20 minutes + 30 minutes baking.
METHOD: Layer fruits in a dish. Mix flour, oats, butter, and sugar to a crumble; sprinkle over fruit. Bake until golden.

9. Watermelon Pizza

INGREDIENTS: Watermelon slice, mixed berries, Greek yogurt, honey, mint.
PREP TIME: 10 minutes.
METHOD: Spread yogurt over watermelon, top with berries, drizzle with honey, and garnish with mint.

10. Kiwi and Strawberry Popsicles

INGREDIENTS: Kiwi, strawberries, coconut water.
PREP TIME: 15 minutes + freezing.
METHOD: Blend fruits with coconut water, pour into molds, and freeze.

Healthy Sweet Treats and Pastries

1. Almond Flour Blueberry Muffins

INGREDIENTS: Almond flour, eggs, honey, baking powder, blueberries.
PREP TIME: 10 minutes + 20 minutes baking.
METHOD: Mix ingredients (except blueberries), fold in berries, bake until golden.

2. Dark Chocolate and Nut Bark

INGREDIENTS: Dark chocolate, mixed nuts (almonds, hazelnuts), sea salt.
PREP TIME: 10 minutes + chilling.
METHOD: Melt chocolate, pour onto parchment, sprinkle with nuts and salt, chill until set.

3. Carrot and Walnut Cookies

INGREDIENTS: Grated carrots, walnuts, oats, honey, egg.
PREP TIME: 15 minutes + 12 minutes baking.
METHOD: Combine ingredients, spoon onto baking sheet, bake until edges are golden.

4. Avocado Chocolate Mousse

INGREDIENTS: Ripe avocados, cocoa powder, honey, vanilla extract.
PREP TIME: 15 minutes.
METHOD: Blend all ingredients until smooth. Chill before serving.

5. Banana and Oat Pancakes

INGREDIENTS: Bananas, eggs, oats, cinnamon.
PREP TIME: 10 minutes + cooking.
METHOD: Mash bananas, mix with eggs and oats, cook like pancakes.

6. Lemon and Poppy Seed Loaf

INGREDIENTS: Almond flour, eggs, honey, lemon zest, lemon juice, poppy seeds.

PREP TIME: 15 minutes + 45 minutes baking.
METHOD: Mix ingredients, pour into loaf pan, bake until a toothpick comes out clean.

7. Coconut and Date Balls

INGREDIENTS: Dates, shredded coconut, almonds.
PREP TIME: 20 minutes.
METHOD: Process dates and almonds, form into balls, roll in coconut.

8. Baked Apples with Cinnamon and Nuts

INGREDIENTS: Apples, nuts (almonds, pecans), cinnamon, honey.
PREP TIME: 10 minutes + 30 minutes baking.
METHOD: Core apples, fill with nut mix, bake until tender.

9. Chia and Berry Pudding

INGREDIENTS: Chia seeds, almond milk, mixed berries, honey.
PREP TIME: 10 minutes + overnight soaking.
METHOD: Mix chia seeds with almond milk and honey, let sit overnight, top with berries.

10. Pumpkin Spice Energy Bites

INGREDIENTS: Pumpkin puree, oats, almond butter, pumpkin spice, chia seeds.
PREP TIME: 15 minutes + chilling.
METHOD: Combine ingredients, form into balls, chill until firm.

Each of these recipes brings a touch of the Atlantic's natural bounty to your dessert table, proving that indulgence and health can go hand in hand. Whether you're craving the fresh zest of fruit or the comforting warmth of a pastry, there's something here to satisfy every palate. Enjoy experimenting, and here's to sweet endings and fresh beginnings!

Chapter 6: Beverages

Welcome to the refreshing conclusion of our culinary journey through the Atlantic Diet. In this chapter, we're diving into the liquid treasures of the Atlantic – from invigorating traditional drinks that have quenched thirsts for centuries, to modern twists on classics, and soothing herbal teas and infusions that offer a warm embrace. Let's raise our glasses to health and happiness with these simple yet delightful recipes.

Traditional and Modern Atlantic Drinks

1. Classic Sangria

INGREDIENTS: 1 bottle of red wine, ¼ cup brandy, 2 tablespoons sugar, orange slices, lemon slices, lime slices, 2 cups sparkling water
PREP TIME: 10 minutes + chilling
METHOD: In a large pitcher, combine the wine, brandy, and sugar. Stir until the sugar is dissolved. Add the sliced fruits and chill for at least 2 hours. Before serving, add the sparkling water for a refreshing fizz.

2. Vinho Verde Spritz

INGREDIENTS: ½ cup Vinho Verde (young Portuguese wine), ¼ cup sparkling water, lime slices, mint leaves
PREP TIME: 5 minutes
METHOD: Fill a glass with ice. Pour in the Vinho Verde and top with sparkling water. Garnish with lime slices and mint leaves for a refreshing twist.

3. Atlantic Rum Punch

INGREDIENTS: ⅓ cup dark rum, ¼ cup orange juice, ¼ cup pineapple juice, 2 tablespoons lime juice, 1 tablespoon grenadine, pineapple slices for garnish
PREP TIME: 5 minutes
METHOD: In a shaker filled with ice, combine all the ingredients except for the garnish. Shake well and strain into a glass filled with ice. Garnish with pineapple slices.

4. Portuguese Lemonade

INGREDIENTS: 4 lemons, peeled and quartered, ¾ cup sugar, 4 cups cold water, fresh mint
PREP TIME: 10 minutes
METHOD: In a blender, combine the lemons, sugar, and 2 cups of water. Blend until smooth. Strain the mixture into a pitcher, add the remaining water, and stir. Serve over ice and garnish with mint.

5. Cider Sangria

INGREDIENTS: 2 cups apple cider, 1 cup ginger beer, ½ cup brandy, apple slices, cinnamon sticks
PREP TIME: 10 minutes + chilling
METHOD: In a large pitcher, mix the cider, ginger beer, and brandy. Add apple slices and cinnamon sticks. Chill for an hour before serving to allow the flavors to meld.

6. Azorean Tea Cooler

INGREDIENTS: 4 cups brewed Azorean green tea (cooled), ¼ cup honey, lemon slices, fresh mint
PREP TIME: 5 minutes + cooling time for tea
METHOD: Brew the tea and let it cool. Once cooled, stir in the honey until dissolved. Serve over ice, garnished with lemon slices and mint.

7. Berry Atlantic Fizz

INGREDIENTS: ½ cup mixed berries (fresh or frozen), 2 tablespoons sugar, 1 cup sparkling water, mint leaves
PREP TIME: 5 minutes
METHOD: Muddle the berries and sugar in a glass until the sugar is dissolved and the berries are broken down. Fill the glass with ice, top with sparkling water, and stir gently. Garnish with mint leaves.

8. Iberian Iced Coffee

INGREDIENTS: 1 cup brewed coffee (cooled), ½ cup milk, 2 tablespoons condensed milk, ice cubes
PREP TIME: 5 minutes

METHOD: In a glass, combine the cooled coffee and milk. Add the condensed milk and stir until well mixed. Add ice cubes and enjoy a sweet, refreshing twist on coffee.

9. Minted Melon Aqua Fresca

INGREDIENTS: 2 cups cubed melon (watermelon, cantaloupe, or honeydew), 1 liter sparkling water, mint leaves, 2 tablespoons lime juice, 2 tablespoons sugar (optional)
PREP TIME: 10 minutes
METHOD: Blend the melon cubes until smooth. Strain the juice into a pitcher, add the lime juice, sugar (if using), and sparkling water. Stir well. Serve over ice and garnish with mint leaves.

10. Seaside Sparkler

INGREDIENTS: ¼ cup blue curaçao, 1 cup white grape juice, sparkling water, ice cubes
PREP TIME: 5 minutes
METHOD: In a glass filled with ice, pour the blue curaçao and white grape juice. Top with sparkling water for a gentle fizz. Stir gently for a beautifully layered effect.

Healthy Herbal Teas and Infusions

1. Atlantic Mint Tea

INGREDIENTS: Fresh mint leaves, 1 teaspoon honey, hot water
PREP TIME: 5 minutes
METHOD: Place a handful of fresh mint leaves in a mug. Pour hot water over the leaves and let steep for 5 minutes. Stir in honey to taste before serving.

2. Lavender and Lemon Balm Tea

INGREDIENTS: 1 tablespoon dried lavender flowers, 1 tablespoon dried lemon balm, hot water
PREP TIME: 5 minutes
METHOD: Mix the lavender and lemon balm in a tea infuser. Place the infuser in a mug and pour hot water over it. Let steep for 5-7 minutes. Enjoy the calming effects of this aromatic blend.

3. Rosehip and Hibiscus Tea

INGREDIENTS: 2 tablespoons dried rosehips, 2 tablespoons dried hibiscus flowers, hot water
PREP TIME: 5 minutes

METHOD: Combine the rosehips and hibiscus in a tea infuser and steep in hot water for 5-7 minutes. This tea is packed with vitamin C and antioxidants.

4. Chamomile and Honey Tea

INGREDIENTS: 2 tablespoons dried chamomile flowers, hot water, 1 teaspoon honey
PREP TIME: 5 minutes
METHOD: Steep the chamomile flowers in hot water for 5 minutes. Strain and add honey to soothe and relax before bedtime.

5. Ginger Turmeric Tea

INGREDIENTS: 1 inch fresh ginger root (sliced), 1 teaspoon turmeric powder, 1 teaspoon honey, hot water
PREP TIME: 10 minutes
METHOD: Boil the ginger slices and turmeric in water for 5 minutes. Strain into a mug and add honey for a spicy immune-boosting drink.

6. Nettle and Peppermint Tea

INGREDIENTS: 1 tablespoon dried nettle leaves, 1 tablespoon dried peppermint leaves, hot water
PREP TIME: 5 minutes
METHOD: Combine nettle and peppermint in a tea infuser. Steep in hot water for 5-7 minutes for a refreshing and detoxifying beverage.

7. Atlantic Seaweed Infusion

INGREDIENTS: 1 tablespoon dried seaw

eed (dulse or kelp), hot water
PREP TIME: 7 minutes
METHOD: Place the dried seaweed in a mug and cover with hot water. Let it steep for 5-7 minutes. Rich in minerals, this infusion is like a taste of the ocean.

8. Fennel and Licorice Root Tea

INGREDIENTS: 1 tablespoon fennel seeds, 1 inch licorice root (sliced), hot water
PREP TIME: 10 minutes

METHOD: Boil the fennel seeds and licorice root in water for 5 minutes. Strain and enjoy a sweet, digestive-friendly tea.

9. Echinacea and Elderberry Tea

INGREDIENTS: 1 tablespoon dried echinacea, 1 tablespoon dried elderberries, hot water
PREP TIME: 5 minutes
METHOD: Steep echinacea and elderberries in hot water for 5-7 minutes. This immune-boosting tea is perfect for cold season.

10. Lemon Verbena and Sage Tea

INGREDIENTS: 1 tablespoon dried lemon verbena leaves, 1 teaspoon dried sage leaves, hot water
PREP TIME: 5 minutes
METHOD: Combine lemon verbena and sage in a tea infuser. Steep in hot water for 5 minutes for a soothing, digestive aid.

Whether you're starting your day with a zesty Atlantic drink or winding down with a calming herbal tea, these recipes are designed to nourish your body and delight your taste buds. Each sip is a reminder of the Atlantic's abundant gifts, so take a moment to savor the flavors and the health benefits they bring. Cheers to your wellness journey!

BONUS: The Atlantic Diet 30-Day Meal Plan

Introduction to Week 1: Embracing Atlantic Flavors

This first week is designed to gently introduce you to the vibrant flavors and health benefits of the Atlantic Diet. You'll enjoy a variety of seafood, fresh fruits and vegetables, whole grains, and healthy fats, such as olive oil. Each day includes three meals: breakfast, lunch, and dinner, with an emphasis on simplicity, nutrition, and taste.

Day 1

Breakfast: Scrambled Eggs with Spinach and Whole Grain Toast
- Start your day with protein-rich eggs, iron-packed spinach, and a slice of whole grain toast.
Lunch: Tuna Salad with Mixed Greens
- A light and refreshing salad featuring tuna, mixed greens, cherry tomatoes, cucumber, and a vinaigrette dressing.
Dinner: Grilled Salmon with Quinoa and Steamed Broccoli
- Enjoy omega-3 rich salmon, served with fluffy quinoa and nutrient-dense steamed broccoli.

Day 2

Breakfast: Yogurt with Honey and Mixed Berries
- A bowl of probiotic-rich yogurt topped with fresh berries and a drizzle of honey for natural sweetness.
Lunch: Chickpea and Vegetable Soup
- A hearty and healthy soup made with chickpeas, carrots, tomatoes, and kale, seasoned with herbs.
Dinner: Baked Cod with Roasted Mediterranean Vegetables
- Cod fillets baked to perfection, served alongside a medley of roasted Mediterranean vegetables like zucchini, bell peppers, and eggplant.

Day 3

Breakfast: Oatmeal with Almonds and Banana
- Start your day with heart-healthy oatmeal, topped with sliced bananas and a sprinkle of almonds.
Lunch: Avocado and Shrimp Salad
- A satisfying salad featuring ripe avocados, grilled shrimp, mixed greens, and a lime dressing.
Dinner: Chicken and Vegetable Stir-Fry
- A simple stir-fry with chicken breast, bell peppers, broccoli, and carrots, served over brown rice.

Day 4

Breakfast: Smoothie with Spinach, Pineapple, and Flaxseed
- A refreshing smoothie made with spinach, pineapple, banana, and ground flaxseed for an omega-3 boost.
Lunch: Lentil Salad with Tomatoes and Feta Cheese
- A flavorful lentil salad with cherry tomatoes, cucumber, feta cheese, and a lemon-olive oil dressing.
Dinner: Seared Tuna Steaks with Sweet Potato Mash
- Omega-3 rich tuna steaks, seared and served with a side of creamy sweet potato mash.

Day 5

Breakfast: Whole Grain Toast with Avocado and Poached Egg
- A satisfying breakfast of whole grain toast, topped with smashed avocado and a poached egg.
Lunch: Quinoa and Black Bean Bowl
- A nutrient-packed bowl with quinoa, black beans, corn, avocado, and a cilantro-lime dressing.
Dinner: Grilled Mackerel with Asparagus and Tomato Salad
- Omega-3 rich mackerel grilled and served with roasted asparagus and a fresh tomato salad.

Day 6

Breakfast: Greek Yogurt Pancakes with Blueberries
- Light and fluffy pancakes made with Greek yogurt, served with fresh blueberries and a hint of maple syrup.
Lunch: Mediterranean Chickpea and Quinoa Salad
- A delicious salad combining chickpeas, quinoa, cucumbers, tomatoes, olives, and feta cheese, dressed in olive oil and lemon juice.
Dinner: Roast Chicken with Potatoes and Green Beans
- A comforting meal of roast chicken, served with roasted potatoes and steamed green beans.

Day 7

Breakfast: Berry and Chia Seed Pudding
- A nutritious pudding made with chia seeds, almond milk, and mixed berries, refrigerated overnight.
Lunch: Tomato and Basil Bruschetta
- Classic bruschetta with fresh tomatoes, basil, garlic, olive oil, on top of toasted whole grain bread.
Dinner: Seafood Paella
- A flavorful paella with a mix of seafood, including shrimp and mussels, cooked with saffron-infused rice and vegetables.

Continuing with the theme of simplicity, nutrition, and variety, here are meal ideas for Days 8 through 14 of the Atlantic Diet 30-Day Meal Plan. These suggestions build on the foundation of the first week, introducing new recipes and ingredients to diversify your diet and continue your exploration of Atlantic flavors.

Day 8

Breakfast: Pear and Walnut Oatmeal
- Warm oatmeal served with sliced pears, walnuts, and a dash of cinnamon.
Lunch: Roasted Beet and Goat Cheese Salad
- A vibrant salad featuring roasted beets, mixed greens, goat cheese, and walnuts, dressed with a balsamic vinaigrette.
Dinner: Grilled Sea Bass with Lemon Herb Quinoa
- Sea bass fillets grilled to perfection, served with lemon and herb-infused quinoa.

Day 9

Breakfast: Avocado Toast with Tomato and Egg
- Whole grain toast topped with smashed avocado, sliced tomato, and a hard-boiled egg.
Lunch: Carrot and Ginger Soup
- A soothing soup made with carrots, ginger, onions, and vegetable stock, blended until smooth.
Dinner: Baked Haddock with Olive Tapenade and Steamed Green Beans
- Oven-baked haddock fillets topped with a homemade olive tapenade, alongside steamed green beans.

Day 10

Breakfast: Smoothie Bowl with Spinach, Mango, and Chia Seeds

- A nutrient-packed smoothie bowl with spinach, mango, banana, topped with chia seeds and coconut flakes.
Lunch: Mediterranean Tuna Wrap
- Whole grain wraps filled with tuna salad, lettuce, cucumber, and olives, dressed with yogurt sauce.
Dinner: Quinoa Stuffed Bell Peppers
- Bell peppers stuffed with a flavorful mix of quinoa, black beans, corn, tomatoes, and spices, baked until tender.

Day 11

Breakfast: Greek Yogurt with Granola and Fresh Fruit
- A bowl of Greek yogurt topped with crunchy granola and your choice of fresh fruit.
Lunch: Spinach and Feta Quiche with a Whole Grain Crust
- A light and tasty quiche with spinach, feta cheese, and eggs, baked in a whole grain crust.
Dinner: Pan-Seared Scallops with Asparagus and Wild Rice
- Tender scallops seared and served with roasted asparagus and a side of wild rice.

Day 12

Breakfast: Banana and Almond Butter Toast
- Whole grain toast spread with almond butter and topped with sliced banana and a sprinkle of chia seeds.
Lunch: Gazpacho
- A refreshing, cold soup made with ripe tomatoes, cucumber, bell peppers, onions, and garlic, served chilled.
Dinner: Lemon Garlic Shrimp with Farro and Arugula Salad
- Shrimp sautéed with lemon and garlic, served over cooked farro and a simple arugula salad.

Day 13

Breakfast: Mixed Berry and Cottage Cheese Parfait
- Layers of cottage cheese, mixed berries, and a sprinkle of granola for crunch.
Lunch: Avocado and Quinoa Salad
- A hearty salad with quinoa, avocado, black beans, corn, and a lime-cilantro dressing.
Dinner: Chicken Tagine with Apricots and Almonds
- A Moroccan-inspired dish with chicken, apricots, and almonds, slow-cooked with spices and served over couscous.

Day 14

Breakfast: Scrambled Tofu with Spinach and Mushrooms
- A vegan twist on scrambled eggs, using tofu scrambled with spinach, mushrooms, and spices.
Lunch: Caprese Sandwich on Whole Grain Bread
- Sliced mozzarella, tomatoes, and fresh basil leaves drizzled with balsamic glaze, sandwiched between whole grain bread.
Dinner: Grilled Sardines with Lemon and Herb Couscous
- Fresh sardines grilled and served with couscous flavored with lemon zest and fresh herbs.

Week 2 Conclusion:
You've now completed two weeks of the Atlantic Diet 30-Day Meal Plan, embracing a variety of flavors and ingredients that promote health and well-being. As you continue on this journey, remember to listen to your body, enjoy the process of cooking and eating wholesome foods, and celebrate the progress you've made towards a healthier lifestyle. Keep exploring new recipes within the "Healthy Atlantic Dishes" cookbook to further diversify your meals and deepen your appreciation for the Atlantic Diet.

Day 15

Breakfast: Pear and Walnut Oatmeal
- Warm oatmeal served with sliced pears, walnuts, and a dash of cinnamon.
Lunch: Grilled Vegetable and Goat Cheese Sandwich
- A delicious sandwich filled with grilled vegetables like zucchini, bell pepper, and eggplant, topped with soft goat cheese on whole grain bread.
Dinner: Lemon Herb Roasted Chicken with Potatoes and Green Beans
- Chicken roasted with lemon, garlic, and herbs, served with oven-roasted potatoes and steamed green beans.

Day 16

Breakfast: Avocado and Tomato on Rye Toast
- Rye toast topped with mashed avocado, sliced tomato, and a sprinkle of salt and pepper.
Lunch: Spinach and Orzo Salad with Feta
- A refreshing salad made with orzo pasta, fresh spinach, cherry tomatoes, olives, and feta cheese, dressed with olive oil and lemon juice.
Dinner: Baked Trout with Almond Crust and Steamed Asparagus
- Trout fillets coated with a crunchy almond crust, baked to perfection and served with lightly steamed asparagus.

Day 17

Breakfast: Mango and Coconut Milk Smoothie
- A tropical smoothie made with fresh mango, coconut milk, and a touch of honey for sweetness.
Lunch: Chicken Caesar Salad with Homemade Dressing
- A healthier take on the classic Caesar, with grilled chicken breast, homemade whole-grain croutons, and a light Caesar dressing.
Dinner: Quinoa Stuffed Bell Peppers
- Bell peppers stuffed with a flavorful mix of quinoa, black beans, corn, tomatoes, and spices, baked until tender.

Day 18

Breakfast: Greek Yogurt with Granola and Pomegranate
- A bowl of Greek yogurt topped with crunchy granola and fresh pomegranate seeds.
Lunch: Mediterranean Tuna Wrap
- A whole-grain wrap filled with tuna, mixed greens, cucumber, olives, and a yogurt-based sauce.
Dinner: Garlic-Lime Shrimp with Brown Rice and Zucchini
- Juicy shrimp sautéed with garlic and lime, served with fluffy brown rice and sautéed zucchini.

Day 19

Breakfast: Spinach and Feta Omelette
- A fluffy omelette filled with fresh spinach and crumbled feta cheese.
Lunch: Lentil Soup with Kale and Carrots
- A hearty and nutritious soup made with lentils, kale, carrots, and aromatic herbs.
Dinner: Pork Tenderloin with Roasted Sweet Potatoes and Brussels Sprouts
- Oven-roasted pork tenderloin served with caramelized sweet potatoes and roasted Brussels sprouts.

Day 20

Breakfast: Banana and Almond Butter Toast
- Whole grain toast spread with almond butter and topped with sliced banana.
Lunch: Quinoa Tabbouleh Salad
- A refreshing salad made with quinoa, parsley, mint, cucumber, tomato, and a lemony dressing.
Dinner: Grilled Sea Bass with Mediterranean Salsa
- Grilled sea bass fillets topped with a salsa made from chopped tomatoes, olives, capers, and herbs, served with a side of grilled vegetables.

Day 21

Breakfast: Berry Quinoa Breakfast Bowl
- A warm breakfast bowl of quinoa topped with mixed berries, a sprinkle of flaxseeds, and a drizzle of honey.
Lunch: Avocado and Egg Salad Sandwich
- A creamy salad of avocado and hard-boiled eggs, lightly seasoned and served on whole grain bread.
Dinner: Moroccan Spiced Chicken with Couscous and Roasted Carrots
- Chicken thighs marinated in Moroccan spices, baked and served with fluffy couscous and honey-roasted carrots.

Conclusion of Week 3
By now, you've explored a wide array of Atlantic Diet-inspired meals, incorporating a balance of seafood, lean meats, whole grains, and plenty of fruits and vegetables. Continue to explore new flavors and ingredients in the weeks ahead, and enjoy the journey towards a healthier, more flavorful lifestyle.

Day 22

Breakfast: Pear and Walnut Oatmeal
- Warm oatmeal with slices of ripe pear, a sprinkle of walnuts, and a dash of cinnamon.
Lunch: Spinach and Orzo Salad
- A refreshing salad with orzo pasta, fresh spinach, cherry tomatoes, and a lemon-olive oil dressing.
Dinner: Baked Trout with Lemon and Dill, Served with Wild Rice
- Oven-baked trout seasoned with lemon and dill, accompanied by a side of aromatic wild rice.

Day 23

Breakfast: Avocado and Egg Breakfast Sandwich
- A hearty sandwich with mashed avocado and a fried egg on whole grain bread.
Lunch: Carrot and Ginger Soup
- A smooth and flavorful soup made with carrots, ginger, and a touch of cream.
Dinner: Grilled Vegetable and Quinoa Salad
- A mix of grilled vegetables (zucchini, bell peppers, eggplant) tossed with quinoa and a balsamic dressing.

Day 24

Breakfast: Banana and Almond Butter Toast
- Whole grain toast topped with almond butter and sliced banana.
Lunch: Mediterranean Tuna Wrap
- A whole grain wrap filled with tuna, mixed greens, olives, and a yogurt-based sauce.
Dinner: Moroccan Chicken Tagine with Apricots and Almonds
- A fragrant dish of chicken cooked with apricots, almonds, and Moroccan spices, served with couscous.

Day 25

Breakfast: Berry Quinoa Breakfast Bowl
- A delightful bowl of quinoa topped with mixed berries, a dollop of Greek yogurt, and a drizzle of honey.
Lunch: Cucumber and Dill Salad with Smoked Salmon
- A fresh cucumber salad with dill and slices of smoked salmon, dressed with lemon juice and olive oil.
Dinner: Seared Scallops with Asparagus and Polenta
- Perfectly seared scallops served with tender asparagus and creamy polenta.

Day 26

Breakfast: Green Smoothie with Spinach, Kiwi, and Flaxseed
- A nutrient-packed smoothie blending spinach, kiwi, banana, and ground flaxseed.
Lunch: Chickpea and Roasted Pepper Salad
- A hearty salad featuring roasted bell peppers, chickpeas, feta cheese, and a garlic-olive oil dressing.
Dinner: Lemon-Garlic Shrimp with Zucchini Noodles
- Shrimp sautéed with lemon and garlic, served over zucchini noodles for a light and healthy meal.

Day 27

Breakfast: Poached Eggs with Avocado and Roasted Tomatoes
- Runny poached eggs served on a bed of avocado slices and roasted cherry tomatoes.
Lunch: Quinoa Stuffed Bell Peppers
- Bell peppers stuffed with a flavorful mix of quinoa, vegetables, and spices, baked until tender.
Dinner: Baked Haddock with Olive Tapenade, Served with Steamed Green Beans
- Oven-baked haddock topped with a homemade olive tapenade, accompanied by steamed green beans.

Day 28

Breakfast: Cottage Cheese with Pineapple and Chia Seeds
- A bowl of cottage cheese topped with fresh pineapple chunks and a sprinkle of chia seeds.
Lunch: Lentil and Sweet Potato Curry
- A comforting curry made with lentils, sweet potato, and coconut milk, served over brown rice.
Dinner: Grilled Swordfish with Mediterranean Salsa
- Grilled swordfish steaks topped with a salsa of tomatoes, olives, and capers.

Day 29

Breakfast: Multigrain Pancakes with Fresh Berries
- Homemade pancakes made with multigrain flour, served with a selection of fresh berries.
Lunch: Avocado and White Bean Wrap
- A whole grain wrap filled with mashed avocado, white beans, arugula, and a squeeze of lime juice.
Dinner: Roasted Chicken Thighs with Lemon and Thyme, Served with Quinoa Salad
- Juicy chicken thighs roasted with lemon and thyme, served alongside a quinoa salad with cucumbers and tomatoes.

Day 30

Breakfast: Chia Pudding with Mango and Coconut
- Overnight chia pudding with almond milk, topped with fresh mango and shredded coconut.
Lunch: Beet and Goat Cheese Arugula Salad
- A vibrant salad of roasted beets, goat cheese, walnuts, and arugula, dressed with a balsamic reduction.

Day 31

Breakfast: Spinach and Feta Omelette
-A fluffy omelette filled with spinach and feta cheese, served with a side of whole grain toast.
Lunch: Cold Pasta Salad with Cherry Tomatoes, Mozzarella, and Basil
- A refreshing pasta salad with cherry tomatoes, mozzarella balls, fresh basil, and an olive oil dressing.
Dinner: Grilled Sea Bass with a Herb Crust, Served with Roasted Mediterranean Vegetables
- Sea bass fillets with a crispy herb crust, grilled to perfection and served with a side of roasted Mediterranean vegetables like zucchini, bell peppers, and eggplant.

This comprehensive meal plan showcases the diversity and health benefits of the Atlantic Diet, focusing on whole foods, seafood, and plenty of fruits and vegetables. Remember to adjust portions and ingredients based on personal preference and dietary needs. Enjoy exploring the flavors of the Atlantic Diet!

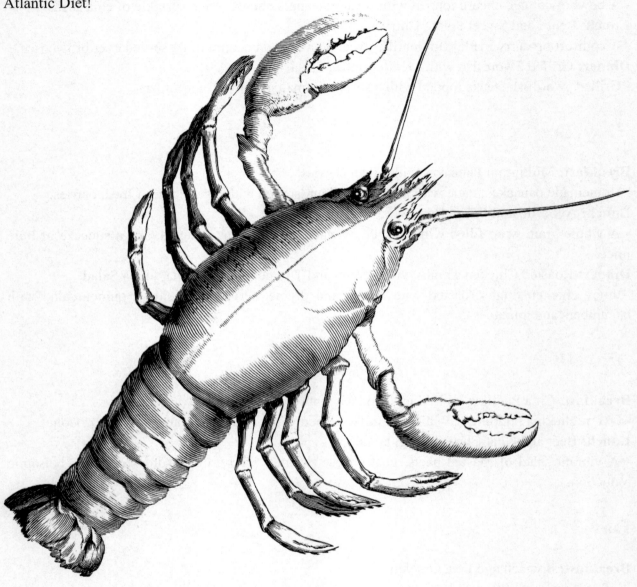

Printed in Great Britain
by Amazon